Decorating Cakes
for Children's Parties

by the same author
Home-Made, and at a fraction of the cost
The Potato Man

Decorating Cakes
for Children's Parties
Polly Pinder

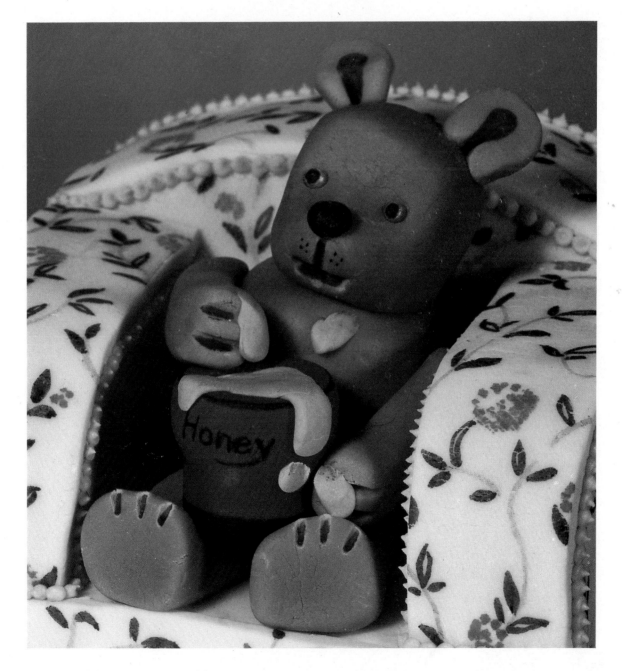

Holt, Rinehart and Winston

New York

Copyright © 1984 by Search Press
All rights reserved, including the right to reproduce
this book or portions thereof in any form.

First published in the United States in 1985 by Holt,
Rinehart and Winston, 383 Madison Avenue, New
York, New York 10017.

Published simultaneously in Canada by Holt,
Rinehart and Winston of Canada, Limited.

Library of Congress Cataloging in Publication Data
Pinder, Polly.
Decorating cakes for children's parties.

Includes index.
1. Cake decorating. 2. Children's parties.
I. Title.
TX771.P56   1985   641.8'653   84–25155
ISBN: 0–03–003667–4

First American Edition
Designer: Polly Pinder
Printed in Spain by Elkar S. Coop, Bilbao-12
Typesetting by EN-TO-EN Ltd., Tunbridge Wells,
Kent, England.

ISBN: 0-03-003667-4

Contents

Introduction

I have to admit that, until being asked to write this book I had never iced a cake in my life . . . a fact which I hope will encourage those who feel that the art of cake decorating is beyond their capabilities. In fact, using fondant icing to decorate cakes is really just a tastier step up from modeling with Plasticine. When our four children were small, I used to spend hours with them at the kitchen table making Plasticine cups, plates, fried eggs, animals and all sorts of little things. Fondant modeling gives even more enjoyment because the "little things" can not only be looked at with delight, but also eaten!

There are thousands of women who relish the thought of their children's parties, the organizing, the preparation and finally the big cake. This book is for them.

For those who have never used the fondant method of decorating before, the best way to approach it is with confidence and a sense of fun. If mistakes are made, they can always be covered up or hidden by a little something made from fondant or royal icing. When I was making the Superman cake (page 82) I did not allow him enough time to dry and as I picked him up to position him on the cake, his arm fell off! After sticking it back on, I made his cape swirl around the arm to cover most of the crack. These things frequently happen but they can usually be easily rectified.

None of the cakes in this book is difficult to decorate but some require more time and patience than others. It is important that you read the general notes first and then read through the step-by-step instructions, perhaps practicing on a "non-celebratory" cake to get used to working with fondant and using an icing bag.

General Notes

The cakes

All the cakes in the book are made from plain rice-cake mixture because, in my experience, children tend to prefer sponge cake to the rich fruit cake recipe normally used for heavy decoration. For this reason the cakes ought to be eaten within a week of being made, because after much longer the sponge will become dry and begin to shrink. There is no reason, however, why the sponge should not be replaced with a rich mixture if you prefer. This book offers a chart, on page 9, which will give you the ingredients and quantities for the size of cake you require.

The plain sponge mixture can be varied in several ways: by adding glacé cherries, chopped walnuts, sultanas, chopped bananas or honey (as a rough guide, if the recipe requires 8oz [220g] of butter, add the same quantity of fruit and nuts); by substituting 1 tblsp of flour and 1 tblsp of rice flour for 2 tblsp of cocoa powder; or by adding extracts—orange, lemon, raspberry, almond, vanilla, etc. The larger cakes can be split and filled with flavored buttercream and/or jam. (If a cake has to be cut into different shapes, it is better to add a flavoring rather than fruit or nuts.)

Method for baking

The method for baking the cakes is this: Beat the sugar and butter until pale and fluffy (substitute margarine for butter if desired); gradually add alternate equal quantities of flour, rice flour and beaten egg and milk. The mixture should have a soft-dropping consistency, a little more milk may be needed in some cases. The cakes are baked in the center of the oven at 350°F (180°C), Gas Mark 4, and are ready when a firm, light-golden crust has formed and the cake has come slightly away from the sides of the pan. Allow to cool in the pan before removing, then leave overnight on a wire rack.

As well as the normal cake pans, food cans are also used to give more variety to the shapes of the cakes. These should be washed, left to dry in a cool oven and then well greased. I cut out (to make releasing the cake easier) the bases and replace them with baking foil, then stand the cans on a baking sheet. They should be just over half filled with mixture and set on a shelf lower than the larger cakes. When the cake is baked, leave it until it is cold, remove the foil, turn a sharp knife around the cake and carefully push it out.

Apricot jam

This is used to coat the cakes before applying the fondant (apricot has the mildest flavor). It should be sieved, to remove skin and hard pieces, and gently heated just prior to brushing a thin film onto the cakes.

Fondant

This is an icing which has liquid glucose added to make it pliable and easy to model. To make 1lb (450g) drop the white of an egg into a bowl and slowly mix in 1lb (450g) of sifted confectioner's sugar and 2 tblsp of warmed liquid glucose. The quantities of confectioner's sugar and egg white are not absolutely critical, more or less of one or the other may be needed to achieve the correct consistency, which should be easy and firm to work with—if it feels floppy, add some more sifted confectioner's sugar; if it becomes hard to handle, add a little more egg white. Some recipes require one quarter of an egg white. As this is difficult to measure, make a rough guess, being generous rather than careful.

Fondant which is not needed immediately should be wrapped in parchment paper or plastic wrap and kept in an airtight container at room temperature, not in the refrigerator.

Ready-made commercial fondant can be bought in ½lb (220g) blocks from cake-decorating specialists and some supermarkets. It is very convenient if you are short of time and it comes in a variety of flavors.

Flavor and color are added to the fondant at the kneading stage, when all the confectioner's sugar and glucose have been mixed in. I would suggest not flavoring the fondant if it has already been added to the

cake mixture. If a pale fondant is required add the color, drop by drop, from a metal skewer. When a large piece of fondant needs to have a very deep color, make a well in the center, pour in the color, then give a shake with the dredger (containing 50% confectioner's sugar and 50% cornstarch) and knead the fondant.

Gum tragacanth (powdered gum) is sometimes used as a hardening agent. Use 1 teaspoon to 8oz (220g) of confectioner's sugar. It is very useful if the fondant is to remain flat, but problems start when you mold and shape round cakes, for it dries rapidly and fine cracks can appear on the surface. The secret is to work very quickly. The gum can be bought from most chemists. It is rather expensive but worth keeping if you intend to do more than one fondant cake.

Spacers

Spacers are used to ensure an even piece of flat fondant. They are placed at each side of the fondant so that the rolling pin rolls over them and the fondant at the same time.

Spacers can be bought from cake-decorating specialists but it is cheaper to buy a packet of flat popsicle sticks (PS) and make your own. These are usually about $\frac{1}{10}$ in. (2mm) thick. Make four spacers (use clear cellophane tape to join the sticks) 4 PS long, the first pair 1 PS thick and the second pair 2 PS thick—see the illustration on this page. Sometimes a piece of fondant needs to be 3 or 4 PS thick. As these pieces are usually quite small the spacers do not have to be long—simply tape the required number together. Again, see the illustration.

Royal icing

To make 8oz (220g) of royal icing, drop one egg white into a very clean bowl (with no traces of grease) and slowly mix in 8oz (220g) of sifted confectioner's sugar. This can be done by hand or in the mixer, using a beater rather than a whisk, on the slowest speed.

Again, the quantities are not critical; you may need more or less of one or the other to obtain the correct consistency. Some recipes need only one-eighth of an egg white. As with the fondant, make a rough guess, erring on the side of generosity. The correct consistency can really only be judged after a little practice with the icing bag—it should not be so runny it loses its shape or so stiff it won't flow easily from the bag.

As with the fondant, add color, drop by drop, from a metal skewer. To obtain a shaded effect of piped work, drop a generous teaspoon of two colored icings, side by side, into the bag.

Royal icing can be stored in an airtight container and kept in the fridge for as long as three weeks, after which it will have to be gently beaten again before being used.

Icing bags and nozzles

I prefer to make my own disposable bags. They are more convenient and easier to use than the commercial tubes and bags, which one has to be continually washing when using different colored icings.

Buy a packet of flat sheets of parchment (rather than a roll). Cut a strip off the sheet to make a square. See the illustration: Fold the square into a triangle; fold point **A** to point **C**; then point **B** to point **D**; then point **C** to point **E**. Snip a small piece from point **X**. Open the bag, drop the nozzle in, making sure that half of it comes out at the bottom. Drop in a couple of teaspoons of royal icing, fold the flap over, fold the two corners **Y** and **Z** inward, then pipe away! As the icing is used, fold the top of the bag over again.

Ateco icing nozzles have been used for all the pipe work on the cakes in this book, but if they are not available in your area you can use the equivalent in another brand—where possible I have drawn the nozzles and the shape produced by each.

You can buy a small nozzle brush—which is extremely useful when you wash the nozzle—from cake-decorating specialists or kitchen equipment shops.

Piped writing

If you have not done piped writing before, it may be as well to practice on the table top.

To pipe onto the iced cake, first write the word on parchment paper, then attach the paper, with two dabs of royal icing, to the cake. Stick a pin at intervals through the pencil lines. Remove the paper. Use the pin marks as guides and the original drawn letters as reference.

To center a word on the cake using a tape measure or ruler, find the center of the cake and mark with a pin. Find the center of the word by measuring, mark with a pencil, then lay the pencil mark over the pin mark.

Coloring

The basic colors can be bought from most supermarkets. For unusual shades you will probably have to go to a cake-decorating specialist. The only *edible* gold and silver I have found comes in powdered form. There is a liquid form sold with other colors of the same brand, but this is labeled toxic and I suggest you do not use it.

Candles

There are candles called "Magic Candles" which relight after being blown out. They are fun, but can be dangerous. I used them for the Rocket (page 86) but we almost had to drown the cake in order to extinguish them.

Steel ruler

This can be bought from cake-decorating specialists and some kitchen equipment shops. It is used to ensure a perfectly flat surface when covering a cake with royal icing—I use it as a straight-edge for cutting fondant.

Small paintbrush

This is useful, not only for color work on models, but for brushing the backs of pieces of fondant, which are then applied to the main cake.

Freezing

I have experimented with the cakes, but freezing is a "hit or miss" way of trying to store them—some areas of the fondant dry, but others become soft and wet. All in all, I would not recommend it.

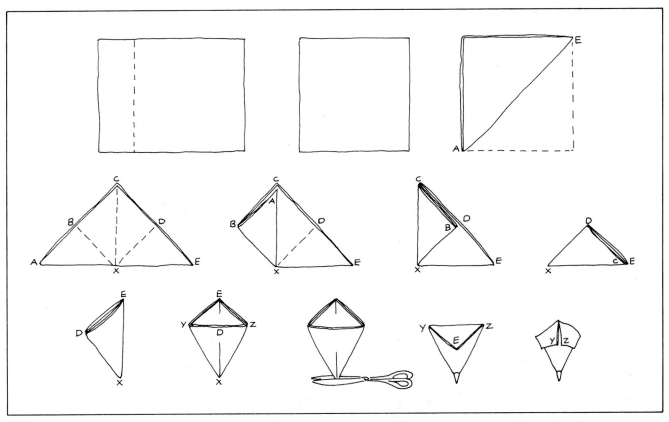

Rich fruit cake

	5in. (130mm) square cake and 6in. (150mm) round cake	6in. (150mm) square cake and 7in. (180mm) round cake	7in. (180mm) square cake and 8in. (200mm) round cake	8in. (200mm) square cake and 9in. (230mm) round cake	9in. (230mm) square cake and 10in. (250mm) round cake	10in. (250mm) square cake and 11in. (280mm) round cake	11in. (280mm) square cake and 12in. (300 mm) round cake
Currants	4oz (110g)	6oz (170g)	10oz (280g)	13oz (360g)	18oz (500g)	24oz (670g)	32oz (900g)
Raisins	3oz (80g)	5oz (140g)	7oz (200g)	10oz (280g)	13oz (360g)	19oz (530g)	22oz (620g)
Sultanas	2oz (60g)	3oz (80g)	4oz (110g)	7oz (200g)	7oz (200g)	13oz (360g)	14oz (390g)
Chopped mixed peel	1oz (30g)	2oz (60g)	2oz (60g)	3oz (80g)	4oz (110g)	5oz (140g)	7oz (200g)
Glacé cherries	1½oz (40g)	2½oz (70g)	3oz (80g)	4oz (110g)	5oz (140g)	8oz (220g)	10oz (280g)
Chopped blanched almonds	1oz (30g)	2oz (60g)	2oz (60g)	3oz (80g)	4oz (110g)	5oz (140g)	7oz (200g)
Grated rind	½ lemon	½ lemon	¾ lemon	1 lemon	1 lemon	1 lemon	1½ lemons
All-purpose flour	3½oz (100g)	6oz (170g)	7½oz (210g)	12oz (340g)	14oz (390g)	21oz (590g)	24oz (670g)
Ground cinnamon	½ teasp	½ teasp	¾ teasp	1 teasp	1½ teasp	2 teasp	2½ teasp
Ground mixed spice	¼ teasp	¼ teasp	½ teasp	¾ teasp	1 teasp	1¼ teasp	1½ teasp
Butter	3oz (80g)	5oz (140g)	6oz (170g)	10oz (280g)	12oz (340g)	18oz (500g)	21oz (590g)
Demerara sugar	3oz (80g)	5oz (140g)	6oz (170g)	10oz (280g)	12oz (340g)	18oz (500g)	21oz (590g)
Medium eggs	1½	2½	3	5	6	9	11
Dark molasses	1 teasp	1 teasp	1 tblsp	1 tablsp	1 tablsp	2 tblsp	2 tblsp
Approx. cooking time	2 hours	2½ hours	2¾ hours	3¼ hours	3¾ hours	4¼ hours	5¼ hours

use first recipe for 2lb (900g) loaf cake

Mary, Mary, Quite Contrary

This is a pretty cake which will charm any little girl.

When buying the silver food color for the bells, be sure to buy the edible sort (it comes in powdered form).

The bowl I use as a base for Mary's dress is slightly smaller than the smallest Pyrex mixing bowl. It holds just under 1pt (560ml) of water and has a diameter of 5in. (125mm).

The cake can be prepared in three days.

Please read the General Notes on pages 6 to 9 before starting to decorate the cake. Also read through the step-by-step instructions and check the ingredients and equipment lists.

Ingredients for cake

16oz (450g) butter
12oz (340g) superfine sugar
20oz (560g) self-rising flour
7oz (200g) rice flour
8oz (220ml) milk beaten with 6 large eggs
filling (optional)

Make from this recipe:
1 × 7in. (180mm) round cake
1 bowl cake

Ingredients for fondant and royal icing

1½lb (670g) confectioner's sugar, plus 6oz (170g)
1½ egg whites, plus ¾
3 tblsp liquid glucose
flavoring (optional)
Also: warm sieved apricot jam; 50/50 mixture of cornstarch and confectioner's sugar in a dusting dredger; green, pink, flesh, blue, yellow and silver food coloring; silver balls.

Equipment

Bowls for mixing icings; sifter; spoons; rolling pin; steel ruler; sharp-pointed knife; popsicle sticks (PS) as spacers; pastry brush; small paintbrush; parchment paper for icing bags; Ateco (or equivalent) icing nozzles 1, 2, 15, 66 and 82; 10in. (255mm) round silver board.

1. Leave the cakes overnight. Slice the tops until the surfaces are completely flat. Turn the round cake upside down and position it in the center of the silver board.

2. Make the fondant. Reserve 8oz (220g) and color the remainder pale green. Measure across round cake. Roll fondant to 2 PS thick and cut a circle to cover cake. Brush cake with warm jam. With help of rolling pin apply fondant.

3. Break off a piece of white fondant. Roll to 1 PS thick. Measure height of bowl cake. Cut a piece to fit—about 4¼in. (110mm) at widest part, as shown. Brush area to be covered with jam and apply fondant.

4. Brush top of bowl cake with jam. Take a piece of green fondant weighing about 3oz (80g). Model top of dress and body in two separate pieces, as shown.

5. Take a piece of white fondant. Color it bright pink. Roll to 1 PS thick and cut a strip 1in. (25mm) wide to fit bottom edge of panel. Apply with egg white, smoothing top edge of pink fondant into the white. Cut a white strip, same width, to go above pink. Cut a fancy edge with cookie cutter.

6. Continue adding a little more pink to strips. Work four fancy pink strips in all, then finish with a white one, wider than the others, for the top of the dress.

Take some white fondant and add flesh coloring. Model a head and neck and attach to body with egg white. Leave both cakes to dry overnight.

7. Position Mary on cake, toward back. Add a little blue to some white fondant. Roll to 1 PS thick. Make gathered part of dress in two pieces, as shown. Brush beneath waistline with egg white. Attach one rectangle of fondant, gathering into waist. Repeat with other piece—gathers will be smooth if fondant is soft.

8. Take a little more white fondant and color it flesh. Model two arms, attach them to body with egg white. Bend arms around slightly to support flowers. With a little green or blue fondant, model two small rectangles for sleeves. Attach around arm tops with egg white.

9. Take another small piece of fondant (any color) and make into a roll. Lay across arm, securing with egg white. Model a little hat from a circle of remaining pink fondant. Attach to head with egg white.

10. With *No. 2 nozzle* pipe white decoration around edge of bonnet. Pipe edging on layers of pink dress and a line of dots at bottom edge. With *No. 1 nozzle* and blue icing, pipe zigzag line around edge of blue dress and on sleeve edges. Pipe tiny dots underneath pink layers and on white icing of bonnet, as shown.

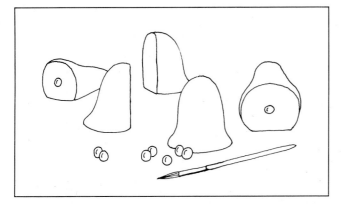

11. Using fondant trimmings, model little bells with a flat side to go against side of cake. Attach a silver ball underneath each, securing with egg white. Leave to dry for 20 minutes, then attach to sides of cake with a dab of icing. Paint with silver coloring.

12. Take a ball of white fondant, mix in silver to make gray. Roll into lengths about 3in. (80mm) long, tapering at both ends. Curl around as shown. Leave to dry for 20 minutes, then attach to sides of cake with a dab of icing.

13. With *nozzle No. 1* pipe pale yellow hair. Paint little blue eyes and red lips on the face. With *nozzle 82* pipe thick green stems for bells and shells. With darker green and *nozzle 2* pipe finer stems on sides of cake and over fondant in Mary's arms.

14. With dark green icing and *nozzle 66* pipe leaves coming up from base of cake. With very pale yellow-green and *nozzle 15* pipe clusters of flowers at tops of finer stems and on stems in Mary's arms.

There Was an Old Woman . . .

. . . **who lived in a shoe**, although it might be more accurate to say, "There was an old woman who lived in a hiking boot"! I thought it might be better to have round cakes rather than the loaf cakes normally used for this subject—the finished shoe is not quite as I had intended, but the flat surfaces make it easier to decorate.

The food coloring used for the little children is flesh. This is not available from supermarkets but can be bought at cake-decorating specialists. If you have difficulty obtaining it, use pink with a drop of brown added.

The cake will take three days to prepare. All three components can be split and filled with buttercream.

Please read the General Notes on pages 6 to 9 before starting to decorate the cake. Also read through the step-by-step instructions and check the ingredients and equipment lists.

Ingredients for cake

10oz (280g) butter
8oz (220g) superfine sugar
13oz (360g) self-rising flour
7oz (200g) rice flour

8oz (220ml) milk beaten with 4 large eggs
filling (optional)
Make from this recipe:
   1 × 6in. (150mm) round cake
   2 × 4½in. (115mm) round cakes

Ingredients for fondant and royal icing

1¾lb (790g) confectioner's sugar, plus 4oz (110g)
1¾ egg whites, plus ½
almost 4 tblsp liquid glucose
flavoring (optional)
Also: warm sieved apricot jam; 50/50 mixture of corn-starch and confectioner's sugar in a dusting dredger; yellow, brown, blue, orange, black and flesh food coloring.

Equipment

Bowls for mixing icings: spoons; sifter; rolling pin; steel ruler; sharp-pointed knife; popsicle sticks (PS) as spacers; pastry brush; parchment paper for icing bag; Ateco (or equivalent) icing nozzles 1, 2 and 65; 12in. (300mm) round silver board.

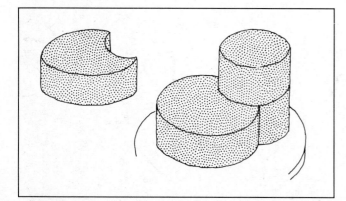

1. Having left the cakes overnight, slice the tops flat. Cut a curved piece out of the large cake, as shown, so that the small cake will fit flush. Sandwich the cakes together with buttercream and/or jam. Position in center of silver board.

2. Make 1¾lb (790g) of fondant. Reserve 5oz (140g) and color the remainder pale brown. Roll to 2 PS thick. Cut circles to fit tops of cakes (cut around baking pans). Brush sponge with warm jam and apply fondant.

3. Measure around tall cake and cut fondant to fit. Apply as before. Measure around large cake and cut fondant to fit. Apply as before, then trim surplus if necessary.

4. Color the remaining fondant with more brown. Roll to 3 PS thick and cut a strip to go around base of shoe ³/₈ in. (10mm) wide (this can be cut in three or four sections). Mark tread with blunt edge of a knife.

5. Model remaining brown to form a tongue, as shown. Brush top and bottom (at back) with egg white and attach to shoe. Let it fall across the joint of the cakes, i.e., do not push it into corner. Leave to dry overnight.

6. Break off some white fondant and color it pale orange. Roll to 1 PS thick. Cut one round window and seven square ones—different sizes. Brush backs with egg white and apply to shoe walls.

7. Break off more white and color pale blue. Model a square chimney. Score a deep line around top, and two lines down each side. Roll a small piece and attach to top. Attach chimney to shoe with egg white. Push candleholder in while fondant is still soft.

8. Roll blue fondant to 1 PS thick. Cut a door and shutters to fit the windows. Score vertical lines with knife, as shown. Brush backs with egg white and apply to shoe. Make small holes in shutters and cut a little heart in the center of the door.

9. Make up the 4oz (110g) of royal icing. Color some dark brown—add black to brown coloring. With icing *nozzle No. 2* pipe circles down each side of the tongue, then pipe laces, crisscross them to and from each hole. Pipe cross-stitch around tops of shoe. Pipe a line of stitching above and below sole of shoe.

10. Color some icing bright orange. With *No. 2 nozzle* pipe around each window. With *No. 1* pipe leading on windows, then pipe around each window again.

11. With *No. 2 nozzle* pipe blue around door and shutters. Pipe hinges and knobs and decoration on chimney. Pipe round heart on door.

12. With *No. 2 nozzle* pipe green stems up the sides of the shoe. Using a different green and *No. 65* pipe leaves on stems.

13. Color the remaining white fondant flesh (or pink with a drop of brown added). Model little children as shown. Put together with egg white while fondant is still fairly soft. Attach to shoe and silver board with egg white.

14. Using *No. 1 nozzle* pipe yellow curly hair on children. Put candle in candleholder.

Hickory Dickory Dock

The only problem with this cake is one of balance. You may notice from the photograph that the clock *leans* slightly—having done all within my power to make it upright, I have convinced myself that the "leaning" adds to the charm, as with the Tower of Pisa!

The cake can be prepared in three days. A little practice on the kitchen table with the icing bag may be necessary if you have not piped before. The filigree can be drawn on to a piece of paper first, the pencil lines are then traced by pricking through them into the fondant, the pin marks being used as a guide. The same technique can be used for the clock numbers and lettering.

Please read the General Notes on pages 6 and 7 before starting to decorate the cake. Also read through the step-by-step instructions and check the ingredients and equipment lists.

Ingredients for cake

10oz (280g) butter
8oz (220g) superfine sugar
13oz (360g) self-rising flour
7oz (200g) rice flour
8oz (220ml) milk beaten with 4 large eggs

buttercream and/or jam for filling
Make from this recipe: 3 × 1lb (450g) loaf cakes—loaf pans measure 3in. × 6in. (75 × 150mm)

Ingredients for fondant and royal icing

1½lb (670g) confectioner's sugar, plus 2oz (60g)
1½ egg whites, plus ¼
3 tblsp liquid glucose
flavoring (optional)
Also: warm sieved apricot jam; 50/50 mixture of corn-starch and confectioner's sugar in a dusting dredger; yellow, blue and pink food coloring; silver balls for decoration.

Equipment

Bowls for mixing icings; spoons; sifter; rolling pin; steel ruler; sharp-pointed knife; popsicle sticks (PS) as spacers; pastry brush; parchment paper for icing bags; Ateco (or equivalent) icing nozzles 1 and 15; 8in. (200mm) square silver board.

1. Having left the cakes overnight, slice the tops flat. Cut cake **A** to 4in. (100mm) long—this will form the base of the clock. Turn cake **B** on its side with the underside facing. Cut cake **C** to 3½in. (90mm) long, turn on its side with underside facing. Join all together with buttercream and/or jam.

2. Make 1½lb (670g) of fondant. Break off 1¼lb (560g) and color it pale blue. Roll to 2 PS thick. Measure back of clock. Cut fondant to fit. Brush sponge with warm jam and carefully apply fondant.

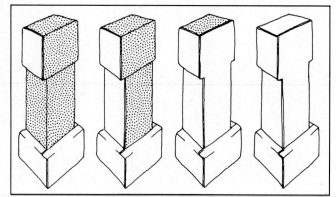

3. Keeping fondant at 2 PS thick, cut and fit all pieces (apply after brushing sponge with warm jam) in following order: top two sides, cutting them long enough to fit under lip; base front, again long enough to fit over base ledge.

4. Cut base sides, as shown, to fit over ledge; cut and fit longest sides, then the front, and finally the top. Leave to dry overnight.

5. Add more blue to remaining fondant. Roll to 1 PS thick and cut a strip ¾ in. (15mm) wide to fit around base of clock. Attach with egg white.

6. With fondant still 1 PS thick, cut a door frame to fit on front of clock. Round off two corners. Cut a fancy strip to go around top of clock—use a cookie cutter for decorative edging, as shown.

7. Model four conical shapes, position on base ledge at each corner. Secure with egg white. Top each with a silver ball. Model four small cones for top of clock. Secure, then add silver balls. Model cones for candles, push candles in while fondant is soft.

8. Break off some white fondant. Roll to 1 PS thick; cut a circle 1¼ in. (30mm) diameter. Color some more white fondant yellow. Cut clockface 2¼ in. (60mm) in diameter and a pendulum $^5/_8$ in. (15mm) in diameter. Apply white circle to clockface. Position pendulum inside door frame. Color remaining white fondant pink.

9. Model the mouse (leave enough fondant for the tail, which can be attached later). Make body from a fat roll, tapering at one end. Make head from a ball, pinching out the ears. Position on top of clock, head overhanging a little. Secure with egg white.

10. Make up the 2oz (60g) of royal icing. With *No. 1 nozzle* and white icing, outline the decorative strip at top of clock. Pipe a narrow zigzag line down side and back seams of fondant. Pipe a line of dots around inside and outside of door frame.

11. Pipe small circles on mouse's head, and gently press in two silver balls. Press a ball in for nose, securing with egg white. Pipe line of dots around cones on base ledge, around base of clock and down front and back seams of base.

12. Pipe the chain holding pendulum and the filigree on door frame. With dark blue icing pipe a line of dots on seam above door. Pipe door hinges as shown and a small circle for handle; press in a silver ball. Pipe numbers and hands on clockface and **Happy Times!** on front of base.

13. Using *No. 15 nozzle* pipe small stars along bottom ledge. Carefully brush back of clockface with egg white and attach to clock.

14. Roll a pink tail for mouse. Attach to body and top of clock, cutting around one of the cones. Stick candles to silver board using egg white.

Humpty Dumpty

Humpty Dumpty, famous for his fall from the wall, can be prepared in three days. The piping is very simple, just straight lines (though these may have to be practiced on the kitchen table if you have not piped before). The two bowls used for making Humpty are 5in. (125mm) in diameter and hold just under 1pt (560ml) of water. Dried fruit can be added to the ingredients as none of the cakes needs to be cut into pieces. Buttercream or jam is used to attach the pudding cakes.

The stone wall can be made to look more realistic by leaving the fondant to dry for about 20 minutes before applying it to the sponge—the surface will develop fine cracks.

Please read the General Notes on pages 6 to 9 before starting to decorate the cake. Also, read through the step-by-step instructions and check the ingredients and equipment lists.

Ingredients for cake

8oz (220g) butter
6oz (170g) superfine sugar
10oz (280g) self-rising flour
6oz (170g) rice flour
3oz (140ml) milk beaten with 3 large eggs
filling
dried fruit or flavoring (optional)
Make from this recipe: 2 pudding cakes
   1 × 2lb (900g) loaf cake

Ingredients for fondant and royal icing

2lb (900g) confectioner's sugar, plus 2oz (60g)
2 egg whites, plus ¼
2 tblsp liquid glucose
flavoring (optional)
Also: warm sieved apricot jam; 50/50 mixture of corn-starch and confectioner's sugar in dusting dredger; blue, red, yellow, black and green food coloring.

Equipment

Bowls for mixing icings; spoons; sifter; rolling pin; steel ruler; sharp-pointed knife; popsicle sticks (PS) as spacers; pastry brush; small paintbrush; parchment paper for icing bag; Ateco (or equivalent) icing nozzle 2; 10in. (250mm) square silver board.

1. Having left the bowl cakes overnight, slice the tops off so that the surfaces are flat. Slice the top and one of the long sides from the loaf cake. Stand loaf cake on its side, in the center of the silver board.

2. Make 1lb (450g) of fondant. Color half of it cream (drop of blue and red with a little yellow) and the other half pale blue. Measure bowl cakes over round surface. Roll cream fondant to 2 PS thick, then cut a circle to fit. Brush sponge with jam and carefully apply fondant, smoothing the surface with your hands.

3. Repeat with the other cake and blue fondant. If edges need trimming, stand cake on overturned bowl and carefully slice away excess—keep trimmings for arms and legs.

4. Make another 1lb (450g) of fondant. Break off 12oz (340g) and add black coloring—mix only partially to give streaky effect. Roll to 2 PS thick. Measure front and sides of wall, cut one piece of fondant to fit. Leave to dry for 20 minutes.

5. Brush cake with jam and apply fondant. Measure back and top. Roll fondant to 2 PS thick and cut fondant to fit. Apply as before. Score horizontal lines all around wall, then vertical lines to form stones. Leave everything to dry overnight.

6. Using a dry paintbrush, lightly brush a corner of each stone in the wall with black coloring to give it texture. Sandwich the two bowl cakes together with buttercream and/or jam. Stand Humpty on dusted parchment paper.

7. Color remaining white fondant red, roll to 2 PS thick. Measure circumference of Humpty and cut a belt to fit, ¾in. (20mm) wide. Brush back of belt with egg white and carefully attach around his middle.

8. Roll fondant to 2 PS thick. Cut a circle and model into shape of a cap. Attach to head with egg white. (If you have one, a tiny dish can be used as a mold for the cap; I use one belonging to a tea strainer.)

9. Roll fondant to 1 PS thick. Cut three buttons, pierce holes with skewer. Brush backs with egg white and attach below belt. Add more red and a little blue to remaining fondant and model a bow tie. Attach front of belt with egg white.

10. Break off some of the remaining blue fondant and model a nose. Roll some of cream fondant to 1 PS thick, cut out eyes, then add smaller circles in blue. Roll a strip of cream for mouth. Attach all the pieces to the face, using egg white.

11. With blue coloring, paint in eyes and a line along the mouth. Position Humpty on wall, using egg white to secure. Roll cream fondant to form two legs, flatten the feet slightly. Attach them to body and wall with egg white.

12. Roll blue fondant to form two arms. Attach to body and edge of wall with egg white. Mark fingers with blunt side of knife. Break off some of remaining gray fondant, add red, and mold around top of arms to make sleeves.

13. Break off more of remaining gray fondant and form into little rocks. Stick them to board with egg white. Poke candles into larger rocks. Make up the 2oz (60g) of royal icing. Pipe pink icing down Humpty's sleeves and a line of pink on each shoe.

14. Pipe red lines on belt and lines going to center of hat, ending with a blob in the middle. Pipe a line on each side of buttons. Pipe a double strap on each shoe and a tiny button on the pink icing. Pipe green grass along bottom edge of wall, in crevices and around some of the stones on the board.

Music

Recorder and Music

For those children who play the recorder at school, this cake will be a special treat. You could even score their favorite tune on the sheet of music!

The cake itself is easy to decorate, but putting the lining in can be a little awkward—the fondant must be very soft because the folds and gathers will crack if it has been handled or rolled out too much. The lid has to be left until completely hard—about two days and nights—before being attached to the case. The cake takes four days to prepare.

Please read the General Notes on pages 6 to 9 before starting to decorate the cake. Also read through the step-by-step instructions and check the ingredients and equipment lists.

Ingredients for cake

6oz (170g) butter
4oz (110g) superfine sugar
8oz (220g) self-rising flour
4oz (110g) rice flour

4oz (110ml) milk beaten with 2 large eggs
Make from this recipe: 2 × 1lb (450g) loaf cakes

Ingredients for fondant and royal icing

1¼lb (560g) confectioner's sugar, plus 2oz (60g)
1¼ egg whites, plus ¼
just under 3 tblsp liquid glucose
flavoring (optional)
Also: warm sieved apricot jam; 50/50 mixture of corn-starch and confectioner's sugar in a dusting dredger; blue, brown, red, black and silver food coloring.

Equipment

Bowls for mixing icings; spoons; sifter; rolling pin; steel ruler; sharp-pointed knife; popsicle sticks (PS) as spacers; wooden spoon; pastry brush; parchment paper for icing bags; Ateco (or equivalent) icing nozzles 1, 2, 3 and 15; 10in. (255mm) square silver cake board.

1. Leave the cakes overnight, then slice the tops flat. Trim two of the narrow sides so that the cakes fit flush. Make the 1¼lb (670g) of fondant. Take a piece and roll to 1 PS thick. Brush the cut sides of cake with warm jam, then sandwich fondant in middle. Push the two cakes together.

2. Take another piece of fondant. Roll to 1 PS thick and cut two oblongs 4¾in. (120mm) long, 3½in. (90mm) wide. Dust a working surface and the wooden spoon handle with dusting mixture.

3. Carefully lay one of the fondant oblongs across handle. Lay the other on top at an angle. Leave them to dry for at least 24 hours.

Cut an oblong in the cake, as shown. Carefully scoop out sponge to ¾in. (20mm) deep. Blow out all crumbs and position cake, on a slant, on silver cake board.

4. Reserve a little white fondant, then color the remainder blue. Measure length and width of cake. Roll a piece to 2 PS thick, cut a lid for the case and five strips for inside lid. Leave to dry for 1 hour.

5. Brush backs of strips with egg white and carefully attach to inside lid, as shown. Dust a surface with dusting mixture and leave lid to dry for at least 48 hours.

Measure sides of cake, including top edge. Brush cake with warm jam. Roll fondant to 2 PS thick and cut to fit. Apply sides first, then front and back.

6. Keep a piece of blue fondant for lid support, add brown to remainder. Model the recorder in separate pieces as shown, keeping a check on length.

7. Make holes while the fondant is still soft. The top hole beneath mouthpiece is made with a teaspoon handle, other holes are made with a knitting needle or paintbrush handle.

8. Using white fondant, model mouthpiece and center and end pieces, as shown. Leave all the parts to dry for a few hours before sticking together with egg white.

9. Color the remaining white fondant red. Roll to 1 PS thick and cut pieces to line case (use two pieces for each long side, as shown). Brush top edge of inside case with egg white, then carefully apply pieces, gathering to make folds. Cut a piece to fit base.

10. When recorder pieces are dry, assemble and lay in case. Make up the 2oz (60g) of royal icing. Color some red and with *nozzle No. 3* pipe three lines of continuous dots around top edge of lining. Pipe same along edges of strips on lid.

11. Using *No. 2 nozzle* and blue icing pipe lines of continuous dots down the four corner seams of fondant on case. Pipe the handle and catch on top of lid, as shown—when dry paint with silver. With *nozzle No. 15* pipe little flowers on corner of case.

12. When little sheets of white fondant are dry, remove wooden spoon. Using *No. 1* and black icing, carefully pipe staves, treble clefs and notes—start with visible areas of bottom sheet first, then top sheet. Transfer to silver board with a spatula, first dabbing board with egg white.

13. When lid is perfectly dry, roll remaining blue fondant to 4 PS thick and cut a strip $5/8$ in. (15mm) wide. Make a groove down center (with steel ruler or blunt edge of a knife) wide enough to fit edge of lid.

14. Attach strip on back edge of case with egg white. Brush egg white inside groove. Carefully lift lid and place in groove. Hold or support it in position until egg white has dried and the lid can support itself.

Drum

The cake can be prepared in two days. The drumsticks must be left to harden for at least 24 hours. As the cake does not have to be trimmed to a particular shape, dried fruit or nuts can be added to the mixture (see page 6). Alternatively, each of the two cakes can be split in half and filled with jam and/or buttercream.

Please read the General Notes on pages 6 to 9 before decorating the cake. Also read through the step-by-step instructions and check the ingredients and equipment lists.

Ingredients for cake

8oz (220g) butter
6oz (170g) superfine sugar
10oz (280g) self-rising flour
6oz (170g) rice flour
5oz (140ml) milk beaten with 3 large eggs
Make from this recipe: 2 × 6in. (150mm) round cakes

Ingredients for fondant and royal icing

1¾lb (790g) confectioner's sugar, plus 4oz (110g)
1¾ egg whites, plus ½
just under 4 tblsp liquid glucose
flavoring (optional)
Also: warm sieved apricot jam; 50/50 mixture of corn-starch and confectioner's sugar in a dusting dredger; red, green, yellow and brown food coloring.

Equipment

Bowls for mixing icings; sifter; spoons; rolling pin; steel ruler; sharp-pointed knife; popsicle sticks (PS) as spacers; pastry brush; parchment paper for icing bags; Ateco (or equivalent) icing nozzles 1, 2 and 3; 9in. (230mm) round silver cake board.

1. Having left the cakes overnight, slice the tops flat and sandwich together with jam and/or buttercream. Brush with jam. Make the 1¾lb (790g) of fondant. Roll a piece for the top to 2 PS thick (cut around the cake tin). Carefully apply fondant.

2. Measure circumference and height of cake. Roll fondant to 2 PS thick and cut a piece to fit. Lay cake on fondant and roll along. Carefully transfer cake to center of silver board. Measure circumference again. (Reserve 4oz [110g] of the fondant.)

3. Cut remainder in two. Color half red, half green. Roll to 1 PS thick, cut eight strips in each color 2½in. (65mm) long, 1¼in. (30mm) wide. (Work four in each color for base of drum first, then roll out and repeat for top of drum.) Brush backs with egg white and carefully apply.

4. Roll two drumsticks, one red, one green, 6in. (150mm) long. Shape as shown. Leave to dry on a dusted surface for 24 hours. Take remaining white fondant, color it orange (mix red and yellow) and roll to 4 PS thick. Cut a strip ⅜in. (10mm) wide, to go around top of drum. Brush egg white around drum edge, attach strip.

5. Add brown to orange trimmings. Roll to 1 PS thick. Cut sixteen strips ⅜in. (10mm) wide—cut eight pieces 1¼in. (30mm) long and eight pieces 2in. (50mm) long. Brush backs with egg white, position over joints of red and green fondant, shorter strips at bottom, longer strips at top.

6. Make the 4oz (110g) of royal icing. With *No. 3 nozzle* and yellow icing, pipe a line of continuous dots to and from the brown strips, as shown. Go around the cake, then start again with a second line next to the first. Pipe a large dot at top of each strip, as shown.

7. With *No. 2 nozzle* and orange icing, pipe a line of continuous dots inside orange strip on top of drum; three lines on red and green panels, as shown, and a line on base of bottom panels. Pipe a line across each brown strip and a circle on panels, as shown.

8. With *No. 1 nozzle* pipe a tassel on each large yellow dot. Pipe top part first, then the strands—each ending with a dot, then the tie, as shown.

Xylophone

This cake can also be prepared in two days, and as with the previous one, the hammer and bars should be left to dry for at least 24 hours. The cake can have added fruit or nuts, or can be sliced lengthways and filled with jam and/or buttercream.

There should really be eight bars on the xylophone (an observant child will no doubt point this out). Unfortunately the loaf cake is not long enough to accommodate eight and thinner ones would, I think, look rather meager. If comments are made, perhaps you can formulate an imaginative retort!

Please read the General Notes on pages 6 to 9 before starting to decorate the cake. It is a good idea also to read through the step-by-step instructions and check the ingredients and equipment lists.

Ingredients for cake

6oz (170g) butter
4oz (110g) superfine sugar
8oz (220g) self-rising flour
4oz (110g) rice flour

4oz (110ml) milk beaten with 2 large eggs
Make from this recipe: 1 × 2lb (900g) loaf cake

Ingredients for fondant and royal icing

1lb (450g) confectioner's sugar, plus 4oz (110g)
1 egg white, plus ½
2 tblsp liquid glucose
Also: warm sieved apricot jam; 50/50 mixture of corn-starch and confectioner's sugar in dusting dredger; red, blue, yellow, mauve and brown food coloring; twelve edible silver balls.

Equipment

Bowls for mixing icings; sifter; spoons; rolling pin; steel ruler; sharp-pointed knife; popsicle sticks (PS) as spacers; pastry brush; parchment paper for icing bag; Ateco (or equivalent) icing nozzle 3; 9in. (230mm) square silver board.

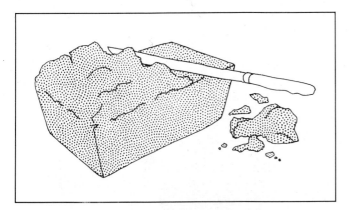

1. Having left the cake overnight, slice the top flat. If desired, slice in half and fill with jam and/or butter-cream.
Make the 1lb (450g) of fondant.

2. Take 12oz (340g) of the fondant and color it green-blue. Measure across cake, then brush it with warm jam. Roll fondant to 2 PS thick and lay one side of cake on top. Carefully roll cake over, covering the three sides. Transfer cake to center of silver board.

3. Measure short sides of cake. Roll fondant to 2 PS thick and cut to fit. Carefully apply. Trim if necessary. Make a circle 1in. (25mm) in diameter and about ½in. (10mm) thick. Make a hole in center, as shown.

4. Take pieces of remaining white fondant. Color red, orange, yellow, mauve, pink and green. Roll each piece to 2 PS thick, cut to 3in. (75mm) by 1in. (25mm). Carefully put aside on a dusted surface.

5. Mix all colored and white trimmings together. Roll fondant to 4 PS thick. Cut into six pieces 6in. (50mm) long, ½in. (10mm) wide. Brush backs with egg white and attach to cake, as shown.

6. Add brown to remaining fondant. Roll a handle 5½in. (140mm) long, tapering slightly at one end. Leave to dry on a dusted surface for at least 24 hours.

7. Make the 4oz (110g) of royal icing. Color slightly paler than fondant on cake. Pipe double lines of continuous dots on seams of fondant, then a single line around base and lines down front and back, as shown.

8. Make a slight indent with paintbrush handle, at each end of colored bars. Dab on a little egg white, then drop in a silver ball. Brush tops of bar supports with egg white, then carefully position the bars on top. Attach handle to hammerhead, securing with egg white.

Rock Group

This cake will take three to four days to prepare. Many of the little pieces have to be completely dry before everything can be assembled. My children (ever critical) complained that the members of the group had rather thick legs! This was done to ensure adequate support for those who were carrying guitars.

The stars on the sides of the cake are cut with a cookie cutter, but they can easily be made by cutting around a template of card.

As the cake remains whole, dried fruit or nuts can be added to the recipe; or it can be sliced in half and filled with flavored buttercream.

Please read the General Notes on pages 6 to 9 before starting to decorate the cake. Also read through the step-by-step instructions and check the ingredients and equipment lists.

Ingredients for cake

10oz (280g) butter
8oz (220g) superfine sugar
13oz (360g) self-rising flour
7oz (200g) rice flour
8oz (220ml) milk beaten with 4 large eggs

dried fruit, nuts or filling (optional)
Make from this recipe:
    1 × 8 in. (200mm) square cake

Ingredients for fondant and royal icing

2lb (900g) confectioner's sugar, plus 2oz (60g)
2 egg whites, plus ¼
2 tblsp liquid glucose
flavoring (optional)
Also: warm sieved apricot jam; 50/50 mixture of corn-starch and confectioner's sugar in dusting dredger; yellow, red, orange, blue, green, flesh, brown, black, silver and gold food coloring (mix red & yellow for orange; red, blue & yellow for brown; yellow & blue for green).

Equipment

Bowls for mixing icings; spoons; sifter; rolling pin; steel ruler; sharp-pointed knife; popsicle sticks (PS) as spacers; pastry brush; star cookie cutter; parchment paper for icing bags; Ateco (or equivalent) icing nozzles 1 and 2; 10in. (255mm) square silver cake board.

1. Having left the cake overnight, slice the top flat. Turn over and position it in center of silver board. Make 2lb (900g) of fondant. Color 1¼lb (560g) with red and yellow—partially mix to give streaky effect. Measure dimensions of cake. Roll fondant to 2 PS thick. Brush cake with warm jam. Cut and apply the top.

2. Apply the four sides. Using fondant trimmings, model spotlights from a roll ¾in. (20mm) in diameter, cut five pieces ³/₈in. (10mm) thick. Smooth edges and cut a small piece from one side, as shown. Model three drums, one 2½in. (40mm) in diameter and two ¾in. (20mm) in diameter—all ½in. (13mm) thick.

The Birthday Bunch

3. Roll fondant to 1 PS thick. Cut twelve stars. Paint backs of floodlights with gold and stars with silver. Leave to dry for an hour, then attach three stars to each side of cake with egg white.

4. Take 8oz (220g) of white fondant, form into an oblong and divide, as shown, into eight sections. Form first four sections into balls and color red, blue, green and yellow. Model four pairs of legs, as shown—position one pair sitting, the others standing.

5. Divide next section into four, leave one white, color others orange, green and blue. Model four bodies as shown. Attach to legs with egg white.

6. Color next section flesh. Divide into four, roll each into a head, keeping a tiny piece for nose. Attach noses with egg white. Attach heads to bodies. Color the next section flesh, wrap and put aside.

7. Divide last section in two. Color half brown, half gray. Roll each to 2 PS thick and carefully cut two guitars, as shown. Use trimmings to model two pairs of gray shoes, two pairs of brown, as shown.

8. Using white fondant, roll to 1 PS thick and cut circles to fit tops of drums. Apply with egg white. Cut a circle for cymbal—paint gold when dry. Color more fondant blue, make a seat for drummer. Make five small balls in different colors, attach them to front of spotlights with egg white.

9. Color more fondant black, roll to 2 PS thick and cut six pieces 1¼in (30mm) long to support small drums. Cut a cymbal and microphone support. Taper all at one end as shown. Model a microphone.

10. Take remaining flesh-colored fondant. Divide into eight and model four pairs of arms. Bend two pairs to support guitars and one pair to go across drums. Attach little microphone to last pair. Do not attach to bodies until dry.
Leave everything to dry overnight.

11. Turn little drums upside down and attach three legs to each with egg white. Turn cymbal upside down, attach support on sloping side, as shown. Cut small hole in cake fondant and push in microphone support. Do same with cymbal, when support is dry and secure.

12. Make up the 2oz (60g) of royal icing. With *No. 2 nozzle* pipe yellow hair on two men. Pipe black hair on other two men, then eyes, as shown. Pipe lines on sides of drums, a dot in center of cymbal, details on guitars and a little line down front of each shoe. With *No. 1* pipe **THE Birthday BUNCH** on large drum.

13. Position seat next to cymbal. Attach drummer to seat with egg white. Position drums around drummer, secure with egg white or hidden dabs of icing. Attach arms to men. Position men and feet, secure with smear of icing. Secure guitars in arms with hidden dabs of icing.

14. With *No. 2 nozzle* pipe black wire from microphone and guitar to microphone stem. Pipe red lips on men, then narrow zigzag lines along fondant seams of cake and around base. Position spotlights with a smear of icing.

Games & Sport

Chess Set

This chess set with movable men will take three to four days to prepare, depending on how quickly you can get into the swing of modeling the separate pieces. It also takes a little time to get the squares of the board to fit correctly without large gaps between each. Time and patience will be rewarded, though, when your chess enthusiast sees the cake.

As the cake remains whole for this subject, dried fruit and/or nuts can be added to the recipe. The orange and purple fondant can be given different flavors.

Please read the General Notes on pages 6 to 9 before starting to decorate the cake. Also read through the step-by-step instructions and check the ingredients and equipment lists.

Ingredients for cake

16oz (450g) butter
12oz (340g) superfine sugar
20oz (560g) self-rising flour
12oz (340g) rice flour
10oz (280ml) milk beaten with 6 large eggs

fruit and/or nuts (optional)
Make from this recipe:
   1 × 11in. (280mm) square cake

Ingredients for fondant and royal icing

3lb (1,340kg) confectioner's sugar, plus 8oz (220g)
3 egg whites, plus 1
6 tblsp liquid glucose
flavoring (optional)
Also: warm sieved apricot jam; 50/50 mixture of cornstarch and confectioner's sugar in dusting dredger; orange and purple food coloring.

Equipment

Bowls for mixing icings; spoons; sifter; rolling pin; steel ruler; sharp-pointed knife; popsicle sticks (PS) as spacers; pastry brush; parchment paper for icing bags; Ateco (or equivalent) icing nozzles 2, 15, 22 and 98; 14in. (280mm) square silver board.

1. Having left the cake overnight, slice the top flat. Turn it over and place in center of silver board. Make 1½lb (670g) of fondant. Color 12oz (340g) orange. Roll to 2 PS thick and cut carefully into thirty-two 1¼in. (30mm) squares.

2. Take the remaining fondant and color it purple. Cut another thirty-two squares as before. Roll trimmings from each color into two balls, cover and put aside. Make another 1½lb (670g) of fondant.

3. Brush top of cake with warm jam. Work about ³/₈ in. (10mm) from edges of cake and carefully apply squares. Take 1lb (450g) of the white fondant. Measure cake sides, including top edge, roll fondant to 2 PS thick and cut to fit. Brush cake with jam and carefully apply fondant.

4. Add more white fondant to white trimmings. Cut in half and roll into a sausage ⁷/₈ in. (22mm) in diameter. Cut into slices just less than ³/₈ in. (10mm) thick and form into round-edged squares—work four at a time. Repeat with second half of fondant. Make forty in all.

5. Take some of the remaining orange fondant. Roll into a sausage ½ in. (12mm) in diameter and cut into eight pieces, 1in. (25mm) long. Form into pawns, as shown, working four at a time. Repeat with purple fondant. Stick pawns to white bases with egg white.

6. Take more white fondant, roll to 2 PS thick and cut circles ⁵/₈ in. (15mm) in diameter to fit on top of pawns. Apply with egg white.

7. Roll little orange and purple balls, attach them to top of each pawn. Model the knights (two each color) from sausages ⁵/₈ in. (15mm) in diameter. Roll to a slight taper, then bend a little. Make four triple bases with colored fondant sandwiched in middle, as shown.

8. Stick knights onto bases with egg white. Model ears—take a tiny ball, flatten, then wrap around paintbrush handle (or knitting needle). Leave to dry for 10 minutes, then attach to heads with egg white.

9. Cut the remaining chess men from a roll ⅝in. (15mm) in diameter. All pieces are 1¼in. (30mm) long and taper slightly, except rooks which are 1in. (25mm) long and do not taper. Roll white fondant to 2 PS thick and cut circles ⅝in. (15mm) in diameter. Apply to tops with egg white. Stick men to remaining bases.

10. Make tops for bishops (two each color) from tapered rolls. Add small white ball to top of each. Make tops for rooks from straight rolls. Attach four tiny white pieces to top, as shown.

11. Make tops for kings and queens, tapering slightly. Add two white balls to slightly flattened queens. Make white crosses for kings—roll fondant to 1 PS thick, cut four pieces and stick together as shown. Leave to dry, then make small cut in tops of kings, drop in a dab of egg white, then stick in crosses.

12. With No. 2 nozzle and white icing pipe wavy lines down back of each knight's head, then pipe eyes. Pipe crowns and mitres on kings, queens and bishops, as shown. Pipe circle around tops of rooks.

13. With No. 98 pipe shell line in pale orange on two top adjoining edges of cake. Pipe other two edges in pale purple. With No. 22 pipe line of dark orange flowers around bottom edge below orange shell lines. Pipe dark purple flowers around other two bottom edges.

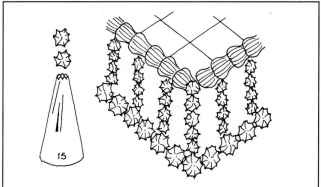

14. With No. 15 pipe white flowers in vertical lines down each side of cake.

Position chess men on board (leave loose, or secure with a smear of icing).

Building Blocks

This edible construction will take three to four days to prepare and build. It would suit a young toddler; or perhaps make an unconventional christening cake by omitting the birthday message and replacing it with the baby's name (the small bricks could each hold a candle for any older brother or sister to blow out).

Please read the General Notes on pages 6 to 9 before starting to decorate the cake. It is also useful to read through the step-by-step instructions and check the ingredients and equipment lists.

Ingredients for cake

10oz (280g) butter
8oz (220g) superfine sugar
13oz (360g) self-rising flour
7oz (200g) rice flour
8oz (220ml) milk beaten with 4 large eggs
Make with this recipe: 1 × 8in. (200mm) square cake

Ingredients for fondant and royal icing

4lb (1,800kg) confectioner's sugar, plus 10oz (280g)
4 egg whites, plus 1¼
8 tblsp liquid glucose
flavoring (optional)
Also: warm sieved apricot jam; 50/50 mixture of cornstarch and confectioner's sugar in a dredger; yellow, pink, blue, green, purple and orange food coloring.

Equipment

Bowls for mixing icings; spoons; sifter; rolling pin; steel ruler; sharp-pointed knife; popsicle sticks (PS) as spacers; pastry brush; parchment paper for icing bags; Ateco (or equivalent) icing nozzles 3, 4, 13 and 15; 14in. (350mm) round silver cake board; small cookie cutter.

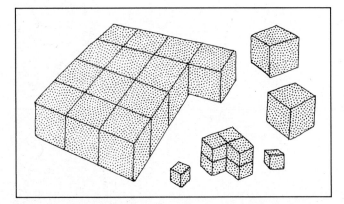

1. Having left the cake overnight, slice the top perfectly flat. Carefully cut into sixteen 2in. (50mm) squares. Cut one of these into eight small squares, as shown.

2. Make the 4lb (1,800kg) of fondant (in two batches). Measure three sides of a large brick, then brush the sides with jam. Roll fondant to 2 PS thick and cut to fit. Place brick on fondant and roll carefully, covering the three sides, as shown.

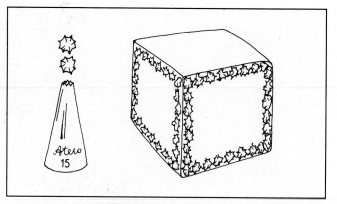

3. Roll a second strip the same size as the first, cover remaining three sides, repeat with all bricks, including little ones. Trim if necessary, so that all edges are perfectly smooth. Leave to dry on a dusted surface overnight.

4. Make the 10oz (280g) of royal icing. With *No. 15 nozzle* pipe stars along seams and down corners of each large brick, as shown. Pipe three bricks with pink, three with pale blue, three yellow, three pale green and three pale purple. Push required number of candleholders into a pink brick.

5. With *nozzle No. 13* and pale orange icing, pipe stars along seams and down corners of small bricks. Using same color and *nozzle No. 3* pipe name of child (if there are enough bricks) or an appropriate message.

6. With *nozzle No. 4* and following the color scheme, pipe **HAPPY BIRTHDAY** on large bricks.

7. Using fondant trimmings, color small pieces, roll to 1 PS thick and cut small flower shapes—four yellow, three pink, three pale green, two pale blue and two pale purple. Brush backs with egg white and apply to appropriate bricks. Leave to dry overnight.

8. Assemble bricks on silver board, as shown. Secure them (including ones actually on board) with smears of royal icing.

Snakes and Ladders

This is a fairly straightforward cake that can be prepared in two and a half days, but some patience is required with the ladders. As the cake is large it might taste better with a filling of flavored buttercream or jam—either slice the whole cake in half, or cut it into nine cubes, smear the filling on each of the cut sides, then press them together again.

Gum tragacanth is added to the fondant that forms the sides of the cake, and it acts as a hardener. The powder can be bought from most pharmacies but it is rather expensive, and unless you intend to do more fondant decorating you may feel it too costly—the cake will survive without it.

Please read pages 6 to 9 before starting to decorate the cake. Also read through the step-by-step instructions and check the ingredients and equipment lists.

Ingredients for cake

16oz (450g) butter
13oz (360g) superfine sugar
20oz (560g) self-rising flour
12oz (340g) rice flour
10oz (280ml) milk beaten with 6 large eggs

filling, flavoring or dried fruit
Make from this recipe:
   1 × 11in. (280mm) square cake

Ingredients for fondant and royal icing

2lb (900g) confectioner's sugar, plus 8oz (220g)
2 egg whites, plus 1
1 teasp gum tragacanth (optional)
4 tblsp liquid glucose
flavoring (optional)
Also: 1lb (450g) marzipan (almond paste); warm sieved apricot jam; 50/50 mixture of cornstarch and confectioner's sugar in a dusting dredger; yellow, red, blue, green and brown coloring; silver balls for decoration.

Equipment

Bowls for mixing icings; sifter; spoons; rolling pin; steel ruler; sharp-pointed knife; popsicle sticks (PS) as spacers; pastry brush; parchment paper for icing bags; fine paintbrush; Ateco (or equivalent) icing nozzles 1 and 15; 14in. (350mm) square silver board.

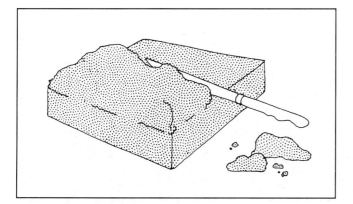

1. Having left the cake overnight, slice the top so that the surface is completely flat. Turn the cake over and position it in center of the silver board.

2. Brush top of cake with the warm sieved jam. Knead marzipan (almond paste), knock into a square, then roll out on a dusted surface to 2 PS thick. Cut around baking pan. Carefully place (with the help of the rolling pin) on top of cake.

3. Make 2lb (900g) fondant. Take just over 1½lb (670g), add gum tragacanth and flavor if desired, then color pale green-blue. Brush sides of cake with jam. Roll fondant to 2 PS thick, cut to size, then apply to cake sides.

4. Roll fondant again to 2 PS thick, cut four strips to fit around top edges of cake, 1in. (25mm) wide. Brush outer area of marzipan with jam, then position fondant strips.

5. Mix leftover trimmings with remaining fondant and divide into three equal portions. Color them red, blue and yellow (because some of the original fondant was colored, you will have subtle shades of red, blue and green).

6. Dust the working surface. Roll fondant to 1 PS thick and cut into neat 1in. (25mm) squares. You will need twenty-seven squares of each color.

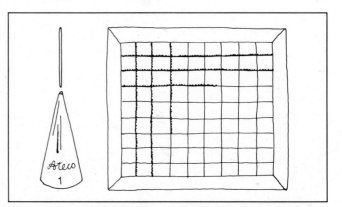

7. Brush a thin film of jam over the marzipan. Carefully position each square as indicated on diagram.

8. Make up the 8oz (220g) of royal icing and keep in an airtight container. Using *No. 1 nozzle* pipe very small white dots along seams of squares.

9. Mix yellow into royal icing. Using *No. 15* pipe small stars around outer edge of colored squares, making a small square at each corner as shown.

10. Pipe one line of stars along top edge of each side. Then, stopping at the square in each corner, pipe one line of stars on joint of fondant and one line at edge of each strip, as shown.

11. Pipe gradating stars on sides of cake as shown, then pipe stars around base of cake.

Add more color to small pieces of fondant. Roll to 1 PS thick and cut round counters. Place in one corner of cake.

12. Add more green to green fondant. Roll five snakes of varying sizes. Flatten heads slightly and bend bodies. Add brown to red fondant. Roll to 1 PS thick and cut into narrow strips. Attach ladder rungs as shown, with a dab of egg white. Leave snakes and ladders to dry.

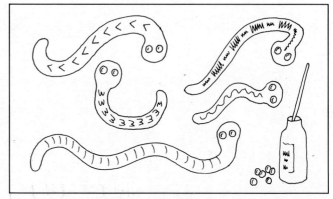

13. Add more blue to remaining blue fondant. Knead, then cut into four cubes. Press in silver balls secured with tiny dabs of egg white. Place a die at each corner of cake, securing with a dab of royal icing. Push candle-holders carefully into dice.

14. Paint patterns with red and blue color on backs of snakes. Pipe two dots of icing on each head and attach silver balls (eyes). Secure ladders and snakes to cake with hidden dabs of icing. Place candles in holders.

Bobsleds

This was originally intended as a ski slope, but after various minor traumas trying to balance the skiers, my son suggested bobsleds. The fact that the sleds are likely to go flying over the edge (as one already has) must be overlooked!

The trickiest part of decorating is applying the white fondant. Fortunately, in order to look realistic, it does not have to be perfectly smooth. I made this cake during the half-term holidays and, because of interruptions by "The Young Pinder Cake-Decorating Advisory Service," it took almost a week to complete. However, it should be done in three or four days.

Please read the General Notes on pages 6 to 9 before starting to decorate the cake. Also read through the step-by-step instructions and check the ingredients and equipment lists.

Ingredients for cake

16oz (450g) butter
12oz (340g) superfine sugar
20oz (560g) self-rising flour
12oz (340g) rice flour
10oz (280ml) milk beaten with 6 large eggs
filling
Make from this recipe: 1 × 11in. (280mm) square cake

Ingredients for fondant and royal icing

3½lb (1.570kg) confectioner's sugar, plus 8oz (220g)
3½ egg whites, plus 1
7 tblsp liquid glucose
flavoring (optional)
Also: warm sieved apricot jam; 50/50 mixture of cornstarch and confectioner's sugar in dusting dredger; red, blue, yellow, green and brown food coloring.

Equipment

Bowls for mixing icings; spoons; sifter; rolling pin; sharp-pointed knife; steel ruler; popsicle sticks (PS) as spacers; pastry brush; parchment paper for icing bags; Ateco (or equivalent) icing nozzles 1, 2, 3 and 41; 11in. (280mm) square silver cake board.

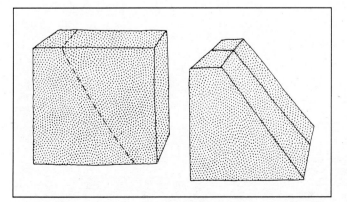

1. Having left the cake overnight, slice the top flat. Measure 1½in. (40mm) from top and bottom opposite sides and cut the cake across, as shown. Join the two pieces with filling (jam or buttercream). Trim if necessary, to make a smooth slope.

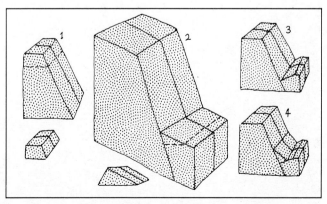

2. Cut 3in. (75mm) off the top. Turn this piece upside down and position at bottom of slope (with filling). Cut a piece out, as shown, and position against main slope, using filling to secure.

3. Make 2lb (900g) of fondant. Take 1lb (450g) and roll to 2 PS thick, roughly the shape of one side of cake. Brush side with jam. Slide cake along table to bottom edge of fondant and lay cake on top of it, jam side down. Cut around fondant and carefully lift cake.

4. Slide cake to another part of table. Brush other side with jam. Roll out fondant and apply as before. Carefully lift cake up, slide to edge of table and onto silver board. Position diagonally.

5. Add more fondant to trimmings. Measure back of slope, then brush with jam. Roll fondant to 2 PS thick and cut to fit. Apply carefully, smoothing with hands. Measure facing front of slope, cut and apply fondant as before.

6. Measure top and entire slope, then brush with jam. Roll fondant to 2 PS thick and cut to fit, in one piece if possible. Carefully apply, then smooth with hands. Mark three pairs of grooves in snow (one pair going off edge) using wooden skewer or knitting needle.

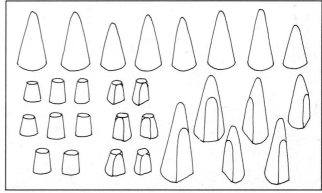

7. Roll more fondant to 2 PS thick. Cut four pieces as shown, to fit around base of cake. Brush bottom edge of cake and part of silver board with egg white. Lay pieces down.

8. Make up the remaining fondant 1½lb (675g)—but use some to complete snow around cake base. Color it green. Make fourteen trees. Color the remaining fondant brown and make fourteen brown trunks, as shown. Slice the backs off six trees and flatten one side of six trunks, as shown—so they can be attached to sides of slope.

53

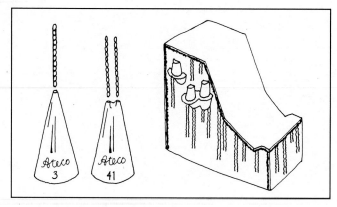

9. Make six shelves to support trees. Model the shapes, brush backs with egg white and attach to cake, two on each side, one at back. Attach trunks to free-standing trees. Position flat-sided trunks on shelves, brushing egg white on base and flat side.

10. Make the 8oz (220g) of royal icing. Using *nozzle No. 3* pipe continuous dots on all cake seams. With *nozzle No. 41* pipe lines down walls to give impression of falling snow.

11. Attach flat-sided trees to trunks and wall of cake. With *nozzle No. 2* pipe green branches on all trees, starting at bottom and working up. Leave free-standing trees to dry, then carefully position on flat snow using egg white to secure.

12. Roll brown fondant to 2 PS thick. Cut three pairs of skis ¼in. (6mm) wide, 3in. (75mm) long, pointed at one end. Leave to dry on dusted surface, support at one end to give a slight curve. Model sleds in red, blue and yellow from a sausage, as shown. Cut pieces out where man is to sit.

13. Model bodies, heads and helmets, as shown, in different colors. Place in sleds, securing with egg white. Position sleds on skis, secure with egg white. Using *No. 2 nozzle* pipe colored markings on sleds. With *No. 1* and brown icing, pipe goggles on men. Leave to dry.

14. Place a lump of white fondant at base of cake, position yellow sled as if fallen (safely) from slope—secure with egg white. Position other sleds as shown, securing lower one with piece of soft white fondant underneath. Gently shake dredger over all the trees.

Football

This subject is made from two cakes. Although both are baked in 11in. (280mm) square tins, the upright cake needs to be thicker than the flat one, so the ingredient quantities are increased. Working with such a large mass of ingredients can be tricky—I first combined the butter and sugar in my blender, then added the remaining ingredients in a dishpan. I then blended everything in two separate batches.

My players appear to be slightly inebriated. This was not intended—although I did leave a glass of wine by the cake one night! One of my teams is the New England Patriots, the other is made up. I suggest you use the colors of your child's two favorite teams.

The cake will take four to five days to prepare.

Please read the General Notes on pages 6 to 9 before starting to decorate. Also read through the instructions and check the ingredients and equipment lists.

Ingredients for cake

1lb (450g) butter
12oz (340g) superfine sugar
20oz (560g) self-rising flour
12oz (340g) rice flour
10oz (280ml) milk beaten with 6 large eggs
Make from this recipe: 1 × 11in. (280mm) square cake

1½lb (670g) butter
1lb (450g) superfine sugar
30oz (840g) self-rising flour
18oz (510g) rice flour
15oz (420ml) milk beaten with 9 large eggs
Make from this recipe: 1 × 11in. (280mm) square cake

Ingredients for fondant and royal icing

5½lb (2.470kg) confectioner's sugar, plus 8oz (220g)
5½ egg whites, plus 1
11 tblsp liquid glucose
flavoring (optional)
Also: warm sieved apricot jam; 50/50 mixture of corn-starch and confectioner's sugar in dusting dredger; green, brown, flesh, yellow, red, blue and silver food coloring.

Equipment

Bowls for mixing icings; sifter; spoons; rolling pin; sharp-pointed knife; steel ruler; popsicle sticks (PS) as spacers; pastry brush; small paintbrush; parchment paper for icing bags; Ateco (or equivalent) icing nozzles 1, 2 and 3; 16in. (400mm) square silver cake board.

1. Having left the cakes overnight, slice the top of the thinner one flat, then turn it over. Stand the thicker cake upright against the other and draw a line, as shown (the pencil mark will be cut away). Lay cake flat and cut out a piece, as shown, cutting just above pencil line.

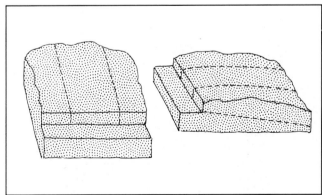

2. Measure 3½in (90mm) in from each side (mark with pencil again) and cut the two side pieces out, sloping toward the top, as shown.

3. Cut the center piece flat, sloping down a little (following natural curve of cake), as shown. Then make a vertical cut in the center piece, as shown, and then cut a slope down to meet the vertical cut, as shown.

Make 2lb (900g) of fondant and color green.

4. Brush top and front of "field" with warm jam. Roll fondant (on well-dusted surface) to 2 PS thick. Lay surface of cake with jam on fondant and cut around three sides. Lift cake onto fourth side to cover, then trim. Carefully position cake toward front of silver board. Paint strokes of green color on top surface.

5. Brush right and left sides of field with jam. Roll fondant to 2 PS thick. Measure each side, cut fondant to fit and carefully apply.

Make 3½lb (1.570kg) of fondant—in two batches for ease. Keep well wrapped.

6. Take 1½lb (670g) of fondant, add it to green trimmings and mix in brown color. Brush top surfaces of carved cake with jam. Measure each surface in turn (apart from top middle surface), roll fondant to 2 PS thick, cut to fit and carefully apply. Brush sides and top of cake with jam and apply fondant as before.

7. Take 1lb (450g) of fondant. Roll a piece to 2 PS thick, cut to fit remaining top middle surface (scoreboard). Brush surface with jam and apply piece of fondant.

Take more white fondant, color some flesh, some darker flesh and some dark brown.

8. Roll about forty-six balls (slightly varying in size) and cut each in half. Make the 8oz (220g) of royal icing. Using *No. 1 nozzle* with black, yellow and red icing, pipe different expressions on faces and different hairstyles as shown. Leave on a dusted surface to dry.

9. Trace the above letters (with child's age) onto parchment paper. Attach paper, with two dabs of white icing, to scoreboard. Stick a pin through pencil lines, then remove. Fill in area made by pin marks with regular dots, as shown.

10. With *No. 3 nozzle* and brown icing, pipe continuous dots on all top surface seams of fondant. With *No. 2 nozzle* pipe fencing, as shown. Pipe double row of dots on middle fence, single row on other two fences. Pipe circles of icing on back of each head and attach to cake.

11. Take remaining brown fondant, add about 4oz (110g) of white. Roll to 1 PS thick. Carefully stand brown cake upright. Brush back with jam, then gently lower onto fondant. Trim around edge, then carefully lift upright again.

12. With *No. 2 nozzle* and white icing, pipe the yard-lines, as shown. Pipe team colors on each side of center line. With same nozzle and green icing, pipe continuous dots on fondant seams, along front, around base and down front panel.

13. Smear back edge of field with jam, then pipe lines of icing over jam. Pipe lines underneath protruding center piece of brown cake. Ask someone to hold silver board level with tabletop and carefully slide brown cake to join back of field.

14. With brown icing and *No. 3 nozzle* fill in any gaps at joint of the two cakes, then pipe continuous dots over joint, on all remaining fondant seams and around base of brown cake.

15. Take about 4oz (110g) of white fondant and color flesh. Make eight heads. Add more brown color to some of brown trimmings, make two more heads. Model the football from brown trimmings. Leave all to dry on a dusted surface.

16. Choose your own colors for the following: take some fondant and model eight helmets—roll a ball slightly smaller than heads, flatten and mold around heads. Model eight bodies for the players, as shown. Model two cheerleader bodies, arms, legs and boots, as shown.

17. Model remaining pieces for players, apart from arms and hands. After four hours, stick cheerleaders together using egg white—the arms will have to be supported for a few minutes until secure. Stick boots, legs and trunks of players together, then stick heads to bodies.

18. Model arms and hands and stick to bodies while still fairly soft; they will have to be supported (use a stack of coins) until secure. Leave overnight.

19. Attach all legs to bodies, using icing to secure. With your own color choice and *No. 2 nozzle*, pipe guards on helmets, numbers on back and front of players, stripes down sides of legs, on helmets and boots. Pipe pleats on cheerleaders' dresses and little loops on hems.

20. With *No. 1 nozzle* pipe all eyes. Pipe curly hair on one cheerleader, straight hair on the other. With same nozzle build up white pompoms on each hand of cheerleaders. Pipe red lips and bows in hair. Pipe a yellow band around the ball. Leave to dry for a while, standing players against supports if necessary.

21. Carefully paint the face guards and cheerleaders' pompoms with silver. Position the ball on the field, securing with egg white.

22. Pipe icing onto soles of feet and position cheerleaders at edge of field. Repeat with each player, allowing them to support each other if they look as if they might fall! Lay one player on the field. Push candleholders into top of scoreboard.

Cricket

I have been told by a very keen cricketer (my husband) that "rain stop(s) play" (not enough spaces for good grammar!) is never put up on the scoreboard; but this theme makes a change from the usual cake–cricket field —and is probably more true to life, in England anyway!

As you can see, the players and pavilion are not in proportion; one could make the men smaller, but then detail would be lost. A slight improvement might be to make the windows wider and deeper.

The cake will take three to four days to prepare. The players are very easy; because they are supported by the steps you will not have to wait for each piece to dry before assembling them.

Please read the General Notes on pages 6 to 9 before you start to decorate the cake. Also read through the step-by-step instructions and check the equipment and ingredients lists.

Ingredients for cake

16oz (450g) butter
12oz (340g) superfine sugar
20oz (560g) self-rising flour
12oz (340g) rice flour
10oz (280ml) milk beaten with 6 large eggs
Make from this recipe: 1 × 11in. (280mm) square cake

10oz (280g) butter
8oz (220g) superfine sugar
13oz (360g) self-rising flour
7oz (200g) rice flour
8oz (220ml) milk beaten with 4 large eggs
buttercream for filling
Make from this recipe: 1 × 8in. (200mm) square cake

Ingredients for fondant and royal icing

4½lb (2.020kg) confectioner's sugar, plus 4oz (110g)
3¾ egg whites, plus ½
7½ tblsp liquid glucose
flavoring (optional)
Also: warm sieved apricot jam; 50/50 mixture of cornstarch and confectioner's sugar in dredger; green, red, brown, black, flesh, blue and silver food coloring.

Equipment

Bowls for mixing icings; sifter; spoons; rolling pin; steel ruler; sharp-pointed knife; popsicle sticks (PS) as spacers; pastry brush; small paintbrush; parchment paper for icing bags; Ateco (or equivalent) icing nozzles 1, 2 and 3; 14in. (350mm) square silver cake board.

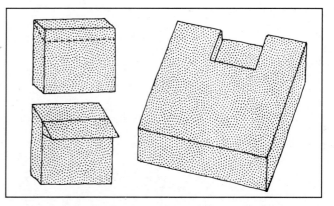

1. Having left the cakes overnight, slice the tops flat. Slice ¾in. (20mm) off one side of smaller cake. Lay this piece flat and cut off a third of it. Cut a 2in. (50mm) piece from the cake. These pieces will form the steps, as shown—the main cake standing a little back from the top step.

2. Slice a sloping piece from top of smaller cake, as shown. This piece will be turned over and attached to continue the sloping roof. Take the larger cake, with smooth base facing up, cut a piece from edge 3½in. (90mm) long, 3in. (75mm) wide, ¾in. (20mm) deep, as shown. Position the cake in center of silver board.

3. Make 1½lb (670g) of fondant and color green. Measure top of large cake, then brush with warm jam. Roll fondant to 2 PS thick, cut to fit and, with help of rolling pin, carefully apply—allow fondant to fall loosely into cutout square.

4. Measure front and sides, then cover with fondant 2 PS thick, as before. Make 2¼lb (1kg) of fondant. Add green trimmings and more green color. Lay largest piece of pavilion on its back. Stick sloping roof on with buttercream.

5. Measure dimensions of roof, front and underneath roof. Brush with jam. Roll fondant to 2 PS thick and cut to fit (front and underneath roof in one piece). Mark planks on roof after application. Leave to dry.

6. Color a small piece of fondant brown. Roll to 1 PS thick, cut door and shutters to fit inside, as shown. Before attaching mark grooves with knife. Paint inside surrounds black, as shown. Roll white fondant to 1 PS thick, cut door and shutters to fit inside, as shown— before attaching mark grooves with knife.

7. Roll green fondant to 1 PS thick. Brush scoreboard (piece taken out of large cake) with jam. Cover back, top and bottom with one piece; cover sides and front with one piece. Leave to dry on dusted surface.

Sandwich steps and pavilion together with buttercream, as shown. Brush steps with jam.

8. Roll fondant to 2 PS thick, measure the three steps in turn, cut fondant to fit, then apply. Brush sides of pavilion with jam. Cut fondant roughly to shape, carefully apply, then trim. Add about 4oz (110g) fondant to green trimmings. Roll to 1 PS thick. Brush back of cakes with jam. Cut fondant to fit, then apply.

9. Make the 4oz (110g) of royal icing. With dark brown icing and *No. 3 nozzle*, pipe continuous dots down edges of roof, along front edge, down sides of front wall and around base of cake. With *No. 2*, pipe continuous dots down sides of steps, around base of bottom step and on all fondant seams.

10. Roll white fondant to 1 PS thick, cut twenty-six posts 1¾ in. (45mm) high, with point at one end. Attach around steps with egg white. Cut horizontal pieces for fence and attach. Cut a step for door and attach.

Make a fourth green step and position between opening of fence.

11. Color some green fondant trimmings black. Make supports for scoreboard. Attach to cake with egg white. Roll black fondant to 1 PS thick, cut oblongs to fit on scoreboard, attach with egg white. With *No.2 nozzle*, pipe **RAIN STOP PLAY** on black pieces. Pipe markings on field as shown.

12. With *No. 1 nozzle* and light brown icing, pipe hinges and knobs on door and shutters, then a hook on each scoreboard letter.

With white fondant model boots, legs (from a roll bent in half), bodies and sleeves. Attach to steps with egg white. Model flesh and brown heads and arms.

13. Attach little noses to faces. Make blue and red caps from flat circles, as shown. Attach to heads. Attach heads to bodies. Paint edging of sweaters, in little dots, as shown, and eyes and lips on faces.

Attach scoreboard to supports with dabs of icing.

14. With *No.2 nozzle* and "runny" white icing, pipe puddles on field, lines down roof and drops on roof edge. After an hour, paint silver. Add a drop of brown to white fondant. Roll to make wickets 1¼ in. (30mm) high. Carefully poke three holes just behind white line. When dry, stick in wickets with egg white.

Alice in Wonderland

"There was a table set out under a tree in front of the house, and the March Hare and the Hatter were having tea at it: a Dormouse was sitting between them, fast asleep . . ."

Of all the charming incidents that occur in the book, this scene is probably the most suitable for cake decorating. The crockery is great fun to make—you may have had practice with your children, using Plasticine. It is important to leave the toadstools as long as possible before positioning the figures on them—they will crack and possibly collapse if they have not had enough time to dry. I have not given the March Hare any legs because with them he would not fit close to the table; he is at the back anyway—but if you prefer to make them, add a little more fondant to the amount given below.

The cake will take three to four days to prepare. Please read the General Notes on pages 6 to 9 before starting. Also read through the step-by-step instructions and check the ingredients and equipment lists.

Ingredients for cake

16oz (450g) butter
12oz (340g) superfine sugar
20oz (560g) self-rising flour
12oz (340g) rice flour
10oz (280ml) milk beaten with 6 large eggs
buttercream for filling
Make from this recipe: 1 × 11in. (280mm) square cake

Ingredients for fondant and royal icing

3lb (1.340kg) confectioner's sugar, plus 4oz (110g)
3 egg whites, plus ½
6 tblsp liquid glucose
Also: warm sieved apricot jam; 50/50 mixture of corn-starch and confectioner's sugar in dusting dredger; red, green, yellow, blue, brown, black, silver and flesh food coloring.

Equipment

Bowls for mixing icings; sifter; spoons; rolling pin; steel ruler; sharp-pointed knife; popsicle sticks (PS) as spacers; pastry brush; small paintbrush; knitting needle or wooden skewer; parchment paper for icing bags; Ateco (or equivalent) icing nozzles 1, 2 and 13; 11in. (280mm) square silver cake board.

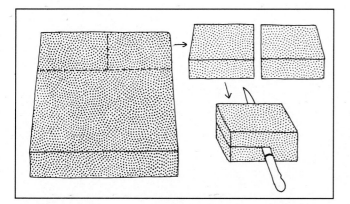

1. Having left the cake overnight, slice the top flat and turn it over. Cut a 7in. (180mm) piece off for the base. Cut the remaining piece in half (this will be the table), then carefully slice one of the halves, as shown.

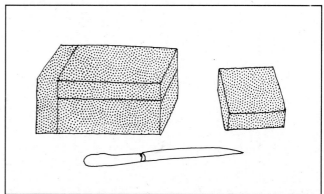

2. Put one of the sliced halves on top of the table to give more height. Cut the remaining piece in half—put one half at side of table to give more length (the rest of that half is extra).

3. Cut the base into four pieces, apply filling, then reassemble. Stick sliced halves to table with filling. Make 1½lb (670g) of fondant and color pale green.

4. Brush top of base with warm jam. Dust working surface liberally and roll fondant 2 PS thick. Lay surface with jam on fondant, then trim away excess. Carefully lift cake and position in center of silver board. Brush away excess powder from surface.

5. Brush sides of base with jam. Measure each in turn, roll fondant to 2 PS thick, cut to fit, then carefully apply. Brush top of table with jam. Roll fondant trimmings to 1 PS thick. Cut to fit and apply, smoothing with hands to make edges round.
   Make another 1½lb (670g) of fondant.

6. Brush underside of table with jam, and position it in center of base. Measure length and width of table, including sides. Color ½lb (220g) of fondant pale yellow. Roll to 1 PS thick and cut to size. Brush tabletop with egg white. With help of rolling pin, apply fondant. Allow folds to fall naturally. Trim.

7. Color 4oz (110g) of fondant red. Divide into four, and model toadstool heads, as shown. Take another 4oz (110g) white fondant, make tiny white flat circles and apply to toadstools with egg white. Make four fat stems with remaining fondant, about 1¾in. (45mm) high and tapering, as shown. Leave to dry.

8. Add more fondant to white trimmings and mix in blue color. Roll fondant to 1 PS thick for plates and saucers. Plates are roughly 1½in. (35mm) in diameter, saucers 1in. (25mm). I used cookie cutters, but use anything of similar size. Cups are solid, and ¾in. (20mm) high. Make grooves in top with wider end of *No. 1 nozzle*.

9. Handles are made from small circles (*No. 12 nozzle* if you have it), 1 PS thick, cut in half and attached to cups and jug with egg white. Make a shallow cavity at top of jug and sugar bowl, then put in white fondant—make rough surface for sugar. Make teapot as shown and assemble, using egg white to secure.

10. Spoons are made from thin strips of fondant 1 PS thick, ¾in. (20mm) long and pressed at one end. Make a small hole in sugar, stick a handle in, securing with egg white. Leave overnight to dry.

Paint blue markings on crockery, as shown. Paint tea in cups. Paint spoons and lid handle with silver.

11. Make the 4oz (110g) of royal icing. With *No. 1 nozzle* pipe underneath each piece of crockery and position on table. Position spoons, using egg white to secure. Again, use piped icing to secure toadstool heads to stems.

12. With *No. 2 nozzle* and pale yellow icing, pipe a line of continuous dots around hem of tablecloth. Position two toadstools at back and as near to table as possible. Secure to base with icing. Position other two at each side, almost at edge of base.

13. Color some fondant flesh and model heads and necks for Alice and the Hatter, as shown. Leave to dry on a dusted surface. With dark brown fondant model pieces for Hare, as shown—curl ears around knitting needle to give deep groove. Attach ears to head after 30 minutes, using egg white. Hold until secure.

14. Flatten two little white balls and attach to head. Color some fondant with drops of black, to make gray mouse. Model head and body in one piece, as shown. Brush base and attach to toadstool while still fairly soft, laying head on plate.

15. Model ears from round circles, bend around end of knitting needle, as shown, and attach to head with egg white. Roll a very thin tail and attach.

Attach Alice's and Hatter's heads to necks, using egg white.

16. Color some fondant green. Form a roll, then pinch out a collar at top. Make a groove down center with knitting needle, then press together. Set aside on a dusted surface.

17. Using orange fondant (mix red and yellow coloring) model Alice's body, pinch out a little collar as before. Model skirt as shown and position on (dusted) edge of working surface. Keep a small piece for sleeves. With dark gray fondant cut a circle 1 PS thick for hat brim, roll a piece for main part. Model shoes, as shown.

18. Using brown fondant, roll Hatter's legs and attach, with shoes, to toadstool. Position body on legs, attach head to body and hat to head. Model arms and position while still fairly soft. Cut a thin oblong of white fondant, attach to hat. Paint black band around hat and over ticket, then paint 10/6 on ticket.

19. Position Alice's skirt on toadstool, using egg white to secure. Attach body to skirt and head to body. Using flesh fondant, model arms, legs and Hatter's hands. Attach while soft. Model sleeves from oblongs, as shown, and attach. Paint details on faces, as shown, and shoes on Alice.

20. With *No.1 nozzle* and white icing, pipe lacy apron on Alice. With *No. 2 nozzle* pipe her yellow hair, in two stages as shown.

With *No.13* and green icing, pipe stars on all fondant seams on base cake.

Winnie-the-Pooh

Winnie-the-Pooh is one of the best-loved characters in children's literature. Here he is indulging once more in his favorite pastime, eating honey.

The cake can be completed in three days. To give a more realistic appearance the chintz design on the chair and tablecloth is painted rather than piped. Pooh himself is modeled from fondant, but almond paste (marzipan) may be used instead—deduct 8oz (220g) of confectioner's sugar and half an egg white from the fondant ingredients and 8oz (220g) of marzipan.

As it is difficult to make a really smooth cut when dried fruit is added to a cake, I suggest you only use a filling for this one.

Please read the General Notes on pages 6 to 9 before starting to decorate the cake. Also read through the step-by-step instructions and check the ingredients and equipment lists.

Ingredients for cake

6oz (170g) butter
4oz (110g) superfine sugar
8oz (220g) self-rising flour
4oz (110g) rice flour
4oz (110ml) milk beaten with 2 large eggs
filling (buttercream)
Make from this recipe: 2 × 5in. (130mm) square cakes

Ingredients for fondant and royal icing

2lb (900g) confectioner's sugar, plus 2oz (60g)
2 egg whites, plus ¼
4 tblsp liquid glucose
flavoring (optional)
Also: warm sieved apricot jam; 50/50 mixture of cornstarch and confectioner's sugar in a dusting dredger; yellow, brown, pink, green, blue and black food coloring; two silver balls for Pooh's eyes.

Equipment

Bowls for mixing icings; spoons; sifter; rolling pin; steel ruler; sharp-pointed knife; popsicle sticks (PS) for spacers; pastry brush; small paintbrush; parchment paper for icing bag; Ateco (or equivalent) icing nozzle No. 2; 10in. (250mm) square silver board.

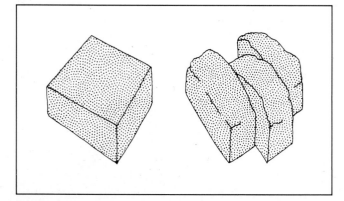

1. Having left the cakes overnight, trim one to form a neat square. Cut middle section out of other cake (leaving a slightly rounded top, which forms back support of chair).

2. The two remaining pieces will form arm rests. Cut a piece from the end of each. Trim these ends into half-circles and join with buttercream to form the little round table.

3. Make 8oz (220g) of fondant (or use equivalent in marzipan). Reserve a small ball for honey, and color the remainder brown. Make Pooh's body from a roll, rounding off edges at top and bottom. Form top surface to slope forward slightly. Stand body on a piece of dusted parchment paper.

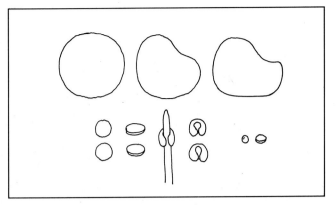

4. Model the head, as shown, from a round ball. Model ears from two small balls—flatten them slightly, then curve around a knitting needle. Make a small ball for the nose and flatten slightly.

5. Make holes for eyes, then press in two silver balls, securing with egg white. Attach ears and nose, secure with egg white. Score mouth as shown, with blunt edge of a knife. Attach head to body using egg white to secure.

6. Model legs and arms from a roll ⅝in. (15mm) in diameter and 6¼in. (160mm) long. Flatten the paws slightly, then form the feet. Score paw marks using blunt edge of a knife. Bend one arm around slightly.
Leave everything to dry overnight.

7. Add a little black and some pink to remaining brown fondant. Model the honey jar. With black coloring paint Pooh's eyes, nose, dots around his mouth, rims around top and bottom of jar, then write **Honey** on jar. Mix brown—pink with a drop of black—and paint inside ears, mouth and paw marks.

8. Color white ball of fondant with yellow and a little brown—for honey. Put some on top of jar, running down sides. Attach legs to body using egg white. Position jar on legs. Attach arms. Smear blobs of honey on paws and on chest.

9. Make 1½lb (670g) of fondant. Color pale yellow. Put chair base on silver board. Roll fondant to 1 PS thick and cut pieces to fit inside arms, inside back and seat of chair. Brush sponge with jam and apply pieces. Attach arms to chair with a film of jam.

10. Roll fondant to 2 PS thick. First cut and apply front of chair, then arm and back tops, then the sides, finally the back.

11. Roll fondant to 2 PS thick, cut a circle slightly larger than the tabletop. Brush sponge with jam and apply fondant, curving over edges of sponge. Roll fondant to 1 PS thick, cut circle about 6in. (150mm) diameter. Place over table, pressing gently in to form folds. Neatly trim edge if necessary.

12. Add pink to remaining yellow fondant. Roll to 1 PS thick and cut four strips 8in. (200mm) long and 1in. (25mm) wide. Gather each strip carefully to each side of chair. Attach with egg white. Trim top of frill straight, then press gently into chair side.

13. Paint chintz design on chair and tablecloth using green, blue and pink coloring. (Follow a reference from a magazine, or copy the simple interpretation above.)

14. Make a square brown cake with fondant trimmings. Apply honey-colored fondant to top, some down the sides. Paint black currants on cake. Attach cake to top of table using egg white.

15. Push candle into cake. Make up the 2oz (60g) of royal icing. Color pink. With *No. 2 nozzle* pipe dots along all chair seams, along top edge of frill and around bottom edge of tablecloth. Place table beside chair on silver board. Carefully position Pooh in the chair.

Tom Sawyer/Huckleberry Finn

I have to confess that, not having read *Tom Sawyer* or *Huckleberry Finn* since childhood, I cannot remember which character sat by a stream with a fishing line tied to his toe. The scene may even be a figment of my imagination—but it feels indicative of the kind of thing both boys would do.

The cake can be prepared in two or three days. Please, before starting, read the General Notes on pages 6 to 9. It is also a good idea to read through the step-by-step instructions and check the ingredients and equipment lists.

Ingredients for cake

12oz (340g) butter
9oz (250g) superfine sugar
15oz (420g) self-rising flour
9oz (250g) rice flour
9oz (250ml) milk beaten with 5 large eggs
buttercream for filling
Make from this recipe:

1 × 6in. (150mm) round cake
1 × 8in. (200mm) round cake

Ingredients for fondant and royal icing

1¾lb (780g) confectioner's sugar, plus 8oz (220g)
1¾ egg whites, plus 1
3½ tblsp liquid glucose
flavoring (optional)
Also: warm sieved apricot jam; 50/50 mixture of cornstarch and confectioner's sugar in a dusting dredger; green, red, black, brown, blue, yellow and silver food coloring.

Equipment

Bowls for mixing icings; sifter; spoons; rolling pin; sharp-pointed knife; popsicle sticks (PS) as spacers; pastry brush; paintbrush; parchment paper for icing bags; Ateco (or equivalent) icing nozzles 1, 2, 13, 66 and 85; 10in. (250mm) square silver cake board.

1. Having left the cakes overnight, slice the tops flat. Cut a piece from smaller cake, as shown, and round off corners—this will be a tree trunk. Sandwich the cakes together with buttercream, small cake toward back of large one. Brush warm jam over both cakes.

2. Make 1¾lb (780g) of fondant. Color 1lb (450g) green. Roll to 2 PS thick and roughly apply to areas shown above—allow fondant to crinkle and crease. Take 4oz (110g) of white fondant, add a line of black color and partially mix to give streaky effect. Make creases in waterfall with knitting needle.

3. Make rough rolls from green trimmings and build up banks of stream, as shown. Add gray trimmings to green and mix in brown color. Brush tree trunk with jam, cover with fondant, modeling gnarled effect and broken branches. Model a narrower trunk with remaining brown fondant. Position trunks as indicated.

4. Add black to remaining trimmings and model rocks, position with egg white as indicated. Color some fondant flesh. Model head and nose, neck, feet and arms—mark fingers and toes with knife. Model red trousers from a roll bent in half, as shown. Attach to cake with feet, using egg white.

5. Model blue body and sleeves, as shown. Position, then fit neck inside body. Add drops of yellow and flesh to a piece of white fondant. Model a hat, marking straw with knife. Attach to head. Roll twigs from brown fondant and build fire, securing with egg white.

6. Make the frying pan—cut small white circle, curve edges up, attach white handle with hole in end, as shown. When dry paint handle brown and pan silver, then position with egg white near fire.

Make the 8oz (220g) of royal icing. With *No. 1 nozzle* and green icing, pipe grass, as shown.

7. With brown icing and *No. 85*, pipe tree trunks up sides of cakes. With dark green and *No. 66*, pipe leaves on trunks. With *No. 2* and paler green, pipe more grasses. Pipe little yellow flowers on grass with *No. 13*. Add a little brown and yellow to remaining white fondant. Roll to 1 PS thick.

8. Cut a 4½in. (120mm) square. Brush tops of trunks and rock with egg white, carefully lay on fondant, turning a corner over on large trunk (support opening until dry). Make a float, position in stream and paint red. With *No. 2 nozzle* and dark icing, pipe a line from toe to float.

Sleeping Beauty's Castle

This cake will take about five days to prepare, so patience is required—but the result is well worthwhile. I recommend it for a very, very special occasion.

The marbling effect on the tiles is obtained by only partially mixing the color (or colors) into the fondant.

If any fondant remains after each session, cover it with parchment paper, keep in an airtight container, then add it to the next batch or use for making small items (a little egg white may need to be added if it has become hard). The conical shapes on which the roof tiles are stuck are not visible, so these can be made from leftovers.

To vary the greens in the piped foliage add a little more yellow or blue, or even a spot of red, to an existing green.

Please read the General Notes on pages 6 to 9 before starting to decorate the cake. Read also through the step-by-step instructions and check the ingredients and equipment lists.

Ingredients for cake

16oz (450g) butter
12oz (340g) superfine sugar
20oz (560g) self-rising flour
12oz (340g) rice flour

10oz (280ml) milk beaten with 6 large eggs
flavoring, filling or dried fruit
Make from this recipe:
    1 × 8in. (200mm) round cake
    1 × 4½in. (115mm) round cake
    1 × 14oz (400g) food-can cake
    4 × 5oz (140g) food-can cakes

Ingredients for fondant and royal icing

3½lb (1.570kg) confectioner's sugar, plus 4oz (110g)
3½ egg whites, plus ½
7 tblsp liquid glucose
flavoring (optional)
Also: warm sieved apricot jam; 50/50 mixture of cornstarch and confectioner's sugar in a dusting dredger; red, blue, yellow, green, brown and black food coloring.

Equipment

Bowls for mixing icings; sifter; spoons; rolling pin; steel ruler; sharp-pointed knife; popsicle sticks (PS); pastry brush; parchment paper for icing bags; fine paintbrush; Ateco (or equivalent) icing nozzles 1 and 15; 14in. (350mm) square silver board.

1. Having left the cakes overnight, slice the tops until they are perfectly flat. Make 1½lb (670g) fondant. Color with drops of red and blue. Roll to 2 PS thick and cut a circle for large cake—then cut from this a circle for the small cake. Coat tops with jam, then cover.

2. Measure around the cakes. Roll fondant to 2 PS thick, then cut to fit. Score horizontal lines using steel ruler. Coat cake sides with jam, then cover. Score vertical lines to form bricks.

Make 1½lb (670g) fondant, color as before.

3. Put one of the small cakes on top of another, securing with jam. Cut four circles to fit tops of cakes (2 PS thick), then cover as before. Measure circumference and height of cakes, cut fondant to fit, and score horizontal lines. Apply fondant and score vertical lines as before. Leave overnight.

4. Position large cake toward the back of the silver board. Position other three cakes as indicated.

Make up the royal icing and store in airtight container.

Add a little egg white (if necessary) and red color to remaining fondant. Knead.

5. Cut steps (A & B) for front and side doors. Position with dabs of royal icing. Cut main steps (D), then cut a double step (C) a little wider. Position as shown. Cut four steps (E) and position.

6. Add a little blue to fondant. Roll to 4 PS thick, then cut about forty squares. Roll fondant again to 2 PS thick and cut another forty squares. Position around tops of two main cakes using dabs of icing to secure. Press required number of candles into fondant while still soft, then remove.

7. Add drops of black to remaining fondant. Roll to 1 PS thick. Cut ten little windows as shown. Brush the backs with egg white and attach where indicated—four go to the back.

8. Add brown to remaining fondant. Roll to 2 PS thick. Cut four doors and score as shown. Brush backs with egg white and attach where indicated.

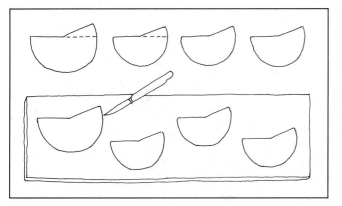

9. Cut from a piece of thin card one circle 7½ in. (190mm) in diameter and three circles 5¾ in. (145mm) in diameter. Cut out wedges as shown. Fold cones around and check that they fit the cakes; they should overhang a little. Using cards as templates, cut one large and three small roofs.

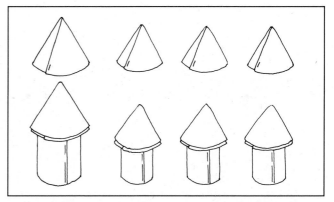

10. Fold templates into cones, secure with staples. Dust outside of cones liberally with cornstarch. Place fondant carefully around each cone. Secure edges with egg white. Stand each cone on a can. Leave overnight. Position the two small cakes ¾ in. (20mm) from front of castle, secure with icing.

11. Make eight icing bags. With *No. 1 nozzle*, two shades of green, pipe grass at intervals around base and top of cakes, on steps, in crevices. *No. 2*, pipe gray down center and around each window. *No. 82*, pipe five brown tree trunks, at back, at each side, by steps, on small castle—continue branches with *No. 3*.

12. With *No. 3* nozzle put two greens in an icing bag and pipe four vine stems—at back, at side, at front and on small castle. *No. 65*, pipe dark green leaves on trees, light green on vines. *No. 1* pipe white flowers (four dots) on trees. *No. 1*, pipe black handles and hinges on doors. Leave to dry overnight.

13. Make ½ lb (220g) marbled fondant. Roll to 1 PS thick and cut roof tiles. Start at bottom edge, stick tiles to fondant cones using egg white. Make four blue balls, flatten slightly, score around edges, then secure to top of roofs with icing. Leave to dry on cans overnight.

14. Smear icing around top edges of each of the four castle parts. Carefully press the roofs into position.

Finally, secure the candles in their holes with a little dab of icing.

Smear a little icing on the undersides of the two small towers and position as indicated.

Adventures

Superman

The idea for this cake was given me by Joseph, my eldest son. I had intended skyscrapers with Superman heroically diving down to save some helpless victim. An ingenious way of suspending him in mid-flight was eluding me, so Joseph's idea was very welcome.

As I have related in the Introduction, Superman's arm fell off because I did not allow him enough time to dry. Twenty-four hours should be sufficient, but he must be handled with great care. Altogether, the cake takes three days to prepare.

Please read the General Notes on pages 6 to 9 before starting to decorate the cake. It is also a good idea to read through the step-by-step instructions and check the ingredients and equipment lists.

Ingredients for cake

10oz (280g) butter
8oz (220g) superfine sugar
13oz (360g) self-rising flour
7oz (200g) rice flour
8oz (220ml) milk beaten with 4 large eggs

Make with this recipe:
    1 × 8in. (200mm) square cake

Ingredients for fondant and royal icing

1¾lb (790g) confectioner's sugar, plus 4oz (110g)
1¼ egg whites, plus ½
just under 4 tblsp liquid glucose
flavoring (optional)
Also: warm sieved apricot jam; 50/50 mixture of cornstarch and confectioner's sugar in dusting dredger; red, blue, yellow, flesh and black food coloring.

Equipment

Bowls for mixing icings; sifter; spoons; rolling pin; steel ruler; sharp-pointed knife; popsicle sticks (PS) as spacers; pastry brush; parchment paper for icing bags and tracing; card; pencil; sewing needle; Ateco (or equivalent) icing nozzles 1, 2 and 3; 10in. (250mm) square silver cake board.

1. Having left the cake overnight, slice the top flat. Make the 1¾lb (790g) of fondant. Color 12oz (340g) blue and 4oz (110g) red, put the red to one side, wrapped. Measure sides of cake, then brush with jam. Roll fondant to 2 PS thick and cut to size.

2. Carefully apply each side, rounding off top edge with hands. Roll trimmings to 1 PS thick and cut a circle roughly 3½in. (90mm) in diameter. Brush area on top of cake with a thin film of jam and apply fondant in center toward back, as shown. Cover the cake with a clean dish towel.

3. Make a card template from the shape given above, then trace the symbol onto parchment paper. Color 1½oz (45g) of fondant yellow, roll to 1 PS thick and cut around template six times. Place tracing over each shape and prick through pencil lines with needle.

4. Make the 4oz (110g) of royal icing. Color about 4 teasp red. With *No. 2 nozzle* pipe lines over needle marks. When all six are complete, add more egg white to icing to make it runny. With *No. 1 nozzle* fill in areas inside lines. Leave symbols to dry for 24 hours on a dusted surface.

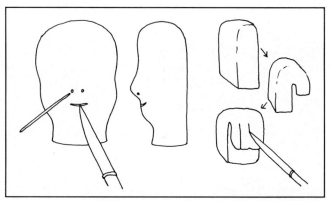

5. Take the remaining blue fondant and model Superman's body and arms, as shown—the body is about 2½in. (65mm) high, the arms 3¼in. (80mm) long. Lay them flat on a dusted surface and attach the arms with egg white.

6. Color a piece of fondant flesh and model a head and neck, in one piece, and hands. Mark nostrils and mouth. Model hands from fat oblongs, bent over to form fists. Mark fingers with blunt edge of knife.

7. Attach head to body and hands to arms. Flatten a small piece of yellow fondant and cut a symbol. Brush back with egg white and attach to chest.

8. With *nozzle No. 2* and red icing, pipe a line around symbol and S inside (this is rather too small to fill in, so use the nozzle like a pencil and fill the letter in as you pipe). Pipe around the mouth. Mix a little blue icing and pipe a line around arm and neck joints. Leave to dry on a dusted surface for at least 24 hours.

9. Color the remaining fondant yellow. Roll to 2 PS thick. Measure top of cake, then brush with jam, apart from blue circle. Apply fondant. Carefully cut a hole for Superman.

10. Smear inside hole with royal icing. Slice Superman onto a spatula and carefully position him in hole. Roll yellow fondant to 2 PS thick and cut wedge shapes. Brush around hole with egg white and attach wedges—Superman has just burst through the cake. Mark cracks on cake with blunt edge of knife.

11. Roll red fondant to 1 PS thick and roughly to shape as shown. Quickly brush back of Superman with egg white and carefully attach cape with a flourish.

12. With *No. 2 nozzle* and black icing, pipe hair and curl on forehead, then eyes and brows. With same nozzle pipe red dots on edge of cape.

13. Roll the remaining red fondant to 1 PS thick. Cut a strip about 6in. (150mm) long and ½in. (12mm) wide. With nozzle No. 2 and yellow icing, pipe **HAPPY BIRTHDAY** (or appropriate message). Cut strip and center the two pieces on cake, using icing to secure.

14. Attach symbols, again using icing to secure—one on each side of cake and two at side of writing. Using *No. 3 nozzle* and red icing, pipe continuous dots along seams of fondant on cake. Push required number of candleholders into back of cake.

Rocket on the Moon

Preparing this cake will take three to four days. Because of the weight of the rocket it is as well to add a little gum tragacanth (see second paragraph on page 47) to the fondant covering the main cake, for it will act as a hardener. (If you do not use it, then make the cake as near as possible to the party day so that the rocket will not sink into the cake and spoil the shape.)

The candles used in the photograph are "Magic Candles," which relight themselves after being blown out. They are great fun but if used it is best to remove them with the holders (bottom ones first) and douse them under the tap—otherwise you may have to throw a bucket of water over the cake!

Please read the General Notes on pages 6 to 9 before starting to decorate the cake. Also read through the step-by-step instructions and check the ingredients and equipment lists.

Ingredients for cake

10oz (280g) butter
8oz (220g) superfine sugar
13oz (360g) self-rising flour
7oz (200g) rice flour
8oz (220ml) milk beaten with 4 large eggs

flavoring, filling or dried fruit
Make from this recipe:
    1 × 8in. (200mm) round cake
    1 × 15oz (420g) food-can cake

Ingredients for fondant and royal icing

2lb (900g) confectioner's sugar, plus 4oz (110g)
2 egg whites, plus ½
4 tblsp liquid glucose
gum tragacanth (if desired)
flavoring (optional)
Also: warm sieved apricot jam; 50/50 mixture of corn-starch and confectioner's sugar in a dusting dredger; blue and green coloring; silver balls for decoration.

Equipment

Bowls for mixing icings; sifter; spoons; rolling pin; steel ruler; sharp-pointed knife; popsicle sticks (PS) as spacers; pastry brush; parchment paper for icing bags; Ateco (or equivalent) icing nozzles 1, 2, 15 and 22; 10in. (255mm) round silver board.

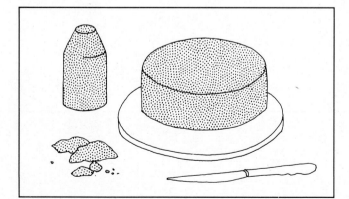

1. Having left the cakes overnight, trim the rocket as shown, sloping at one end and with a flat top. Slice the top of the round cake until it is flat, then position it upside down in center of silver board.

2. Make the fondant, adding flavor if desired. Cut in two, cover one half. (Knead 2 teasp gum tragacanth into remaining half.) Roll to 2 PS thick, then cut circle to cover top and sides of cake. Brush cake with jam, carefully apply fondant, then trim around bottom edge.

3. Place rocket on an overturned saucer, then put the saucer on a small jar or tin so that it can swivel around. Color the remaining half of fondant pale blue. Measure height and circumference of rocket.

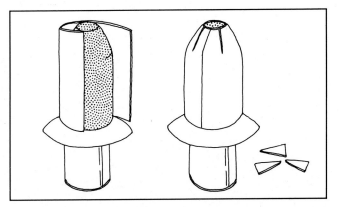

4. Roll fondant to 2 PS thick and cut to size. Brush sponge with jam. Carefully wrap fondant around sponge. Cut out four Vs at top to fit nozzle.

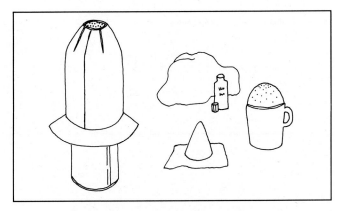

5. Take a little of the blue fondant, add some more blue and model a point for the rocket. Place it on wax paper. Leave everything to dry overnight.

6. Measure circumference of rocket again, roll fondant to 1 PS thick, cut three strips ¾in. (20mm) wide. Brush backs with egg white, then position as shown.

7. Make up the 4oz (110g) of royal icing and keep in an airtight container. Spread a film of jam on top of the rocket, add dabs of royal icing and press on the point of the rocket.

8. Roll blue fondant to 1 PS thick. Cut ten strips ³⁄₈ in. (10mm) wide and attach where indicated on rocket. Cut nine strips to fit on nozzle. Position strips with egg white but avoid seam of fondant at back of rocket. Cut out and attach five round white windows (1 PS thick).

9. Using *No. 2 nozzle* pipe blue lines where indicated. Add silver balls as soon as each line has been piped. Pipe little dots at top and bottom of each line near rocket base. Leave to dry overnight.

10. Carefully transfer rocket to cake (rocket seam underneath). Secure with lines of royal icing and position rough lumps of white fondant (moon rocks) to support—these are secured with dabs of icing.

11. Add more blue to blue fondant and model eight small rockets ½in. (14mm) in diameter and 2¼in. (55mm) long. Roll fondant 2 PS thick and cut a circle to fit rocket base. Coat sponge with jam and apply fondant.

12. Attach little rockets with dabs of icing. Pipe lines where indicated (No. 2) and position silver balls. Using No.15 small star, pipe stars around base seam, on strip seams and at base of point.

13. Position more moon rocks on surface. Model two craters, as shown, and position in front of rocket using egg white to secure.

14. Add green to remaining white fondant, model two heads with big ears, and two arms. Place inside the craters. Stick a pair of antennae on each head with dabs of icing. Mark mouths with a knife.

15. Using No.1 nozzle pipe green eyes, noses and curly hair onto moon-men, then a dot on each antenna. With No.15 pipe pale blue stars on moon surface. Using No. 22 pipe larger stars around base of moon.

Indian Tepee

This cake can be decorated in one day. There will be quite a few spare sponge trimmings when the cake has been cut to shape, so perhaps you will find a use for them—there is usually a hungry-looking child around on baking day, lurking near the kitchen table with an eye on the leftovers and extras!

If your daughter or son has done project work at school on the American Indians, you may have access to genuine Indian symbols and design work. These could be incorporated into the piping on the tepee.

Please read the General Notes on pages 6 to 9 before starting to decorate the cake. Also read through the step-by-step instructions and check the ingredients and equipment lists.

Ingredients for cake

12oz (340g) butter
9oz (250g) superfine sugar
15oz (420g) self-rising flour
9oz (250g) rice flour

9oz (250ml) milk beaten with 5 large eggs
filling
Make from this recipe: 3 x 6in.(150mm) round cakes

Ingredients for fondant and royal icing

1lb (450g) confectioner's sugar, plus 6oz (170g)
1 egg white, plus ¾
2 tblsp liquid glucose
yellow coloring, and flavoring (optional)
Also: warm sieved apricot jam; 50/50 mixture of cornstarch and confectioner's sugar in a dusting dredger; brown, black, red, green and orange food coloring.

Equipment

Bowls for mixing icings; sifter; spoons; rolling pin; sharp pointed knife; popsicle sticks (PS) as spacers; pastry brush; small paintbrush; parchment paper for icing bags; Ateco (or equivalent) nozzles 2, 3 and 41; 9in. (230mm) round silver board.

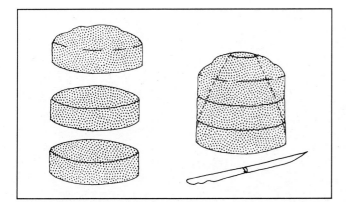

1. Having left the cakes overnight, trim two of the tops until perfectly flat. Stand them on top of one another and cut to a conical shape, leaving a flat surface at the top about 1½in. (40mm) in diameter (very little sponge is sliced from the bottom cake).

2. Carefully take each cake off and fill with jam and/or buttercream. Replace cakes and position them in center of silver board. Cut a triangle out for opening, as shown.

Make 1lb (450g) of fondant. Brush entire cake with warm sieved jam.

3. Color the fondant brown. Roll to 2 PS thick and cut into irregular pieces, as shown. Apply to cake (allow some of the fondant to wrinkle, like buffalo hide). Measure door opening; cut a piece of fondant to fit. Roll fondant to 1 PS thick; cut a circle 1¾in. (45mm) in diameter.

4. Put door and circle aside.
   Add black to brown trimmings. Roll to 2 PS thick and cut a circle for top. Apply. Cut three pieces to line inside opening. Apply. Roll remaining fondant and cut into eight 1¾in. (45mm) lengths. Leave to dry.

5. Brush one edge of opening with egg white and attach door, slightly away from wall of tepee.
   Paint brown lines along seams of fondant on tepee, then paint stitching, as shown.

6. Make the 6oz (170g) of royal icing. With *nozzle No. 3* and yellow icing, pipe a line of continuous dots around top of tepee. With *No. 2* and same color, pipe Ys as shown. Pipe Ws and upturned Vs just above center. Pipe circles, lines, and dots where indicated.

7. Pipe lines on door and bird symbol on the circle of fondant. With *nozzle 41* and pale orange icing, pipe zig-zag lines where indicated. Using green icing and *No. 3 nozzle* pipe Vs and dots as shown and an eye in the bird symbol. Change to *No. 2 nozzle* and deep orange icing.

8. Paint Vs, dots, and lines where indicated and around bird's tail. Paint three brown vertical lines on door. Attach poles, indenting top surface slightly and using egg white to secure. Attach symbol with dabs of icing. Using *No. 3 nozzle* and yellow icing, pipe two more lines of continuous dots around top of tepee.

Early Settlement Fort

Not wishing to introduce violence, I decided to make this a peaceful early settlement fort. Strictly speaking it probably should be a triangular shape, but this would mean less cake to eat! The walls should be much thinner, which would also mean less cake.

The piped lines are easy to manage if you can tip the front of the board up. Gravity will then pull the lines against the wall. The cake can be prepared in two days.

Please read the General Notes on pages 6 to 9 before starting to decorate the cake. It is a good idea also to read through the step-by-step instructions and check the ingredients and equipment lists.

Ingredients for cake

16oz (450g) butter
12oz (340g) superfine sugar
20oz (560g) self-rising flour
12oz (340g) rice flour
10oz (280ml) milk beaten with 6 large eggs

Make from this recipe:
1 × 11in. (280mm) square cake

Ingredients for fondant and royal icing

1½lb (670g) confectioner's sugar, plus 10oz (280g)
1½ egg whites, plus 1¼
3 tblsp liquid glucose
flavoring (optional)
Also: warm sieved apricot jam; 50/50 mixture of cornstarch and confectioner's sugar in a dusting dredger; yellow, brown and black food coloring.

Equipment

Bowls for mixing icings; sifter; spoons; rolling pin; steel ruler; sharp-pointed knife; popsicle sticks (PS) as spacers; pastry brush; parchment paper for icing bags; Ateco (or equivalent) icing nozzles 2, 3 and 7; 14in. (360mm) square silver cake board.

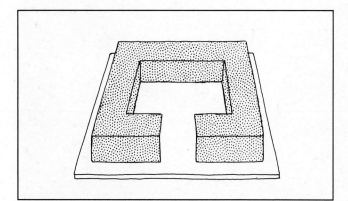

1. Having left the cake overnight, slice the top flat. Cut a 6½in. (165mm) square from the center and a 2in. (50mm) piece from the front, as shown. Carefully turn cake over and position in center of board.

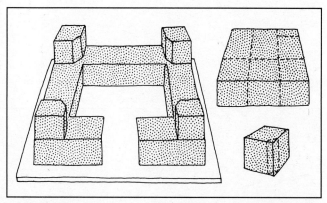

2. Cut the square into three pieces, 2+ × 6½in. Cut four pieces to fit at each corner of fort, with a sliver cut from one corner of each, as shown. Smear bases with jam and/or buttercream, and position, slanting side facing inward.

3. Cut part of remaining sponge into four buildings with sloping roofs. Make the 1½lb (670g) of fondant, color all but a small piece pale brown. Brush inside walls of fort with jam. Measure the walls in turn, roll fondant to 1 PS thick and apply carefully.

4. Brush little buildings with jam. Roll fondant to 1 PS thick. Cover sides first, then cut front, roof and back in one piece. Model a little well, as shown, but do not assemble.

5. Add more brown to fondant. Brush all sponge surfaces of cake with jam. Roll fondant to 1 PS thick. Measure surfaces in turn, cut fondant to fit and carefully apply. Continue until cake is completely covered.

6. Roll fondant to 1 PS thick. Cut five pieces ¼in. (7mm) wide, 2½in. (60mm) long, with a point at one end. Cut three narrow pieces to go across. Leave to dry, then stick cross-pieces to go across. Leave to dry, then stick cross-pieces on with egg white. Set aside.

7. Color the piece of white fondant yellow. Roll to 1 PS thick and cut ten windows of varying size. Brush backs with egg white and apply to buildings and inside walls of fort.

8. Make the 10oz (280g) of royal icing. Leave about three teaspoonsful white and color remainder brown. With *nozzle No. 3* pipe beams on building and inside fort walls, as shown—tip the board up slightly (supporting with a cup or glass) for each facing side.

9. With *No. 2 nozzle* pipe vertical lines around base of well. Pipe a dab of icing in center and attach small support. Dab top of support and attach roof. Pipe beams on both ends of roof.

10. Remembering to tilt board, use the same nozzle to pipe lines inside gateway, on flat surface of each wall, and on inside walls of lookout posts (in that order).

With *No. 7 nozzle* pipe lines on outside walls, again tilting board.

11. Color the remaining white icing ocher (yellow and a drop of brown). With *No. 2 nozzle* pipe irregular lines on roofs of buildings. Finish with a line of continuous dots along ridges.

12. Add black to remaining brown icing. With *No. 2* pipe ladders on sides of lookout towers, as shown. Using *No. 3* pipe continuous dots around top of lookout towers, on edges of walls, down four main corners and around base.

13. Smear the base of each building with icing and carefully position inside the fort.

14. Pipe a line of icing down one side of entrance and attach gate. Stick a candle in each tower (or however many are required) and secure them.

Fun Cakes

Fast-food Addict

Apart from those who have suddenly become weight-conscious, most young people are happy to have fries with everything. This cake would be ideal for those who will eat nothing but fries and the usual accompanying greasy food. A couple of sausages could also be added.

The cake can be prepared in two days. To add more fun, each item of food could have a different flavor —peppermint fries, vanilla egg, strawberry beans, banana hamburger!

Please read the General Notes on pages 6 to 9 before starting to decorate the cake. Also read through the step-by-step instructions and check the ingredients and equipment lists.

Ingredients for cake

8oz (220g) butter
6oz (170g) superfine sugar
10oz (280g) self-rising flour
6oz (170g) rice flour
5oz (140ml) milk beaten with 3 large eggs
filling (optional)

Make from this recipe:
    1 × 8in. (200mm) round cake

Ingredients for fondant and royal icing

1¾lb (790g) confectioner's sugar, plus 1oz (30g)
1¾ egg whites, plus ⅛
almost 4 tblsp liquid glucose
flavoring (optional)
Also: warm sieved apricot jam; 50/50 mixture of cornstarch and confectioner's sugar in a dusting dredger; yellow, blue, green, brown and orange food coloring.

Equipment

Bowls for mixing icings; spoons; sifter; rolling pin; steel ruler; sharp-pointed knife; popsicle sticks (PS) as spacers; pastry brush; small paintbrush; French fry cutter; parchment paper for icing bag; Ateco (or equivalent) icing nozzle 3; 10in. (250mm) round silver board.

1. Having left the cake overnight, slice the top flat. Turn cake over and place in center of silver board. Make the fondant. Measure circumference and height of cake. Roll fondant to 2 PS thick and cut a piece to go around cake. Brush sides with warmed jam. Roll cake onto fondant.

2. Brush top of cake with jam. Roll fondant to 2 PS thick. Cut circle to fit (cut around cake pan). With help of rolling pin apply fondant.

3. When fondant is dry, paint repeating flower design around sides. Make up the royal icing. Pipe a line of continuous dots around top fondant seam.

4. Take 6oz (170g) of fondant. Add brown coloring and a little black. Add more brown and partially mix. Start to shape the hamburger, pinching top to give an uneven surface. Make three grill grooves with paintbrush handle, paint some black in the grooves. Leave to dry, then bend a little to make surface cracks.

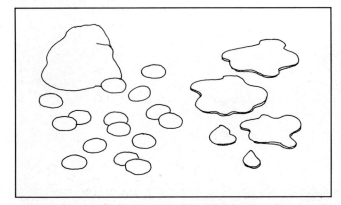

5. Take 3oz (80g) of fondant. Color orange with a little brown. Form into baked beans. Flatten some pieces to make bean sauce. Position hamburger on cake, then put dribbling sauce and beans around hamburger, using egg white to secure.

6. Take 5oz (140g) of fondant. Color it with a little yellow, partially mix in a little brown. Roll to 4 PS thick and cut into fries with French fry cutter. Arrange around back of hamburger, securing with egg white.

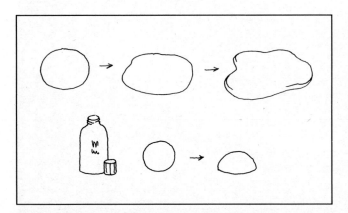

7. Take about 2oz (60g) of fondant. Form white of egg from a ball, flatten and smooth it. Form yellow yolk from a ball, flatten slightly and round off.

8. Position egg white in remaining space on cake, then secure yolk with egg white. Brush hamburger, fries and egg yolk with egg white to give nice greasy finish.

Soap

This very ornate marble soap dish and smooth bar of soap can be given to the young person who is constantly being told by members of the family not to spend all her/his life in the bathroom—or, it can be given to the young person who is persistently being told by his/her parents to "get washed!"

(The theme for the cake was not planned. I had intended a wood-grain finish for another cake, but the resulting marble effect was so interesting, I felt it must be put to use.)

The cake can be prepared in two days.

Please read the General Notes on pages 6 to 9 before starting to decorate the cake. Also read through the step-by-step instructions and check the ingredients and equipment lists.

Ingredients for cake

6oz (170g) butter
4oz (110g) superfine sugar
8oz (220g) self-rising flour
4oz (110g) rice flour
4oz (110ml) milk beaten with 2 large eggs

filling (optional)
Make from this recipe: 1 × 2lb (900g) loaf cake

Ingredients for fondant and royal icing

1½lb (670g) confectioner's sugar, plus 2oz (60g)
1½ egg whites, plus ¼
3 tblsp liquid glucose
flavoring (optional)
Also: warm sieved apricot jam; 50/50 mixture of corn-starch and confectioner's sugar in a dusting dredger; brown, red, black, blue and gold food coloring.

Equipment

Bowls for mixing icings; sifter; spoons; rolling pin; steel ruler; sharp-pointed knife; popsicle sticks (PS) as spacers; pastry brush; small paintbrush; parchment paper for icing bag; Ateco (or equivalent) icing nozzles 3 and 98; 10in. (250mm) square silver board.

1. Having left the cake overnight, slice the top so that the surface is perfectly flat. Cut small pieces from the center edges at front and back, as shown. Turn cake upside down and place in center of silver board.

2. Make 1½lb (670g) of fondant. Take about 8oz (220g), color it pale blue and form a smooth oval —some confectioner's sugar may have to be kneaded into the fondant so that the shape does not flop. Form indent in top of soap with finger when the shape is perfectly smooth. Leave to dry on dusted surface.

3. Take a small piece of fondant, about 1oz (30g), and color it rich brown, adding some red and a little black. The five pieces of fondant covering the cake have each to be worked with a fresh piece of white so that the marble effect is not lost.

4. Brush cake with warmed jam. Take a piece of white fondant, form into a flat oblong and dab with small pieces of brown. Knead very lightly, then roll to 2 PS thick. Cut to fit front of cake, easing fondant into recess on top edge.

5. Repeat with sides and back, then top, easing fondant into recess and smoothing with finger so that the joint cannot be seen.
Make the 2oz (60g) of royal icing.

6. With icing *nozzle No. 8* pipe white scrolls on corners of cake. With *No.* pipe three curved lines under scrolls on each side. Pipe lines of continuous dots down the corners, along top edges and around base.

7. Pipe four dots in center of front and back base lines. Pipe a solid line around recess, then another line inside, as shown, with a dot at each end. Pipe a small line in center over the two lines, ending with a dot. Repeat with recess at back.

8. When piped icing has dried, paint scrolls and lines on recess, as shown, with gold coloring. Position soap on slab. Secure, if desired, with egg white.

Shoe Polishing Kit

This is specifically for the child who constantly frowns at the request to polish his (usually boy's) shoes. A very young child might not understand (or might even be a little hurt) by the cake, but an older child of 12 or 13, with a sense of humor, will appreciate the message.

The most time-consuming part of decorating is taken up by piping of the brush bristles. Everything else is quite straightforward and the cake can be prepared in three days.

I suggest that dried fruit not be added to the cake as it has to be cut up and the pieces of fruit may distort the shapes.

Please read the General Notes on pages 6 to 9 before starting to decorate the cake. It is also useful to read through the step-by-step instructions and check the ingredients and equipment lists.

Ingredients for cake

16oz (450g) butter
12oz (340g) superfine sugar
20oz (560g) self-rising flour
12oz (340g) rice flour
11oz (310ml) milk beaten with 6 large eggs
flavoring, or filling, for main cake
Make from this recipe:
   1 × 11in. (280g) square cake

Ingredients for fondant and royal icing

2½lb (1.120kg) confectioner's sugar, plus 8oz (220g)
2½ egg whites, plus 1
5 tblsp liquid glucose
Also: 8oz (220g) marzipan; warm sieved apricot jam; 50/50 mixture of cornstarch and confectioner's sugar in a dredger; red, yellow, green and brown food coloring.

Equipment

Bowls for mixing icings; sifter; spoons; rolling pin; steel ruler; sharp-pointed knife; popsicle sticks (PS) as spacers; pastry brush; parchment paper for the icing bags; Ateco (or equivalent) icing nozzles 1, 2 and 3; 11in. (280mm) square silver board.

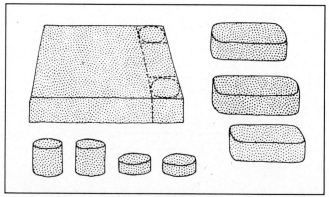

1. Having left the cake overnight, cut off a 2¼in. (56mm) slab—cut from this a 4in. (100mm) piece and a 4½in. (115mm) piece—trim the small remaining square into a circle, then slice it in two (see diagram).

2. Cut another slab 1¾in. (45mm) wide. Cut from this two squares, then trim them into circles. The remainder of the slab will be a brush. Trim all pieces, including the main cake, so that surfaces are flat. Round off the corners of the brushes.

3. Roll marizpan to 2 PS thick. Cut to fit top of large cake. Brush cake with jam and apply marzipan.

Make 1½lb (670g) of fondant. Color it pale green. Roll to 2 PS thick. Measure cake sides and cut fondant to fit. Brush sides with jam. Carefully apply fondant.

4. Add more green to fondant. Roll to 4 PS thick. Cut into four ½in. (15mm) wide strips. Attach to top edges of cake using egg white to secure.

5. Add brown and a little red to fondant. Roll to 2 PS thick. Cut pieces to fit round cakes (jars of shoe polish). Brush cakes with jam. Apply to tops and bottoms first, then the sides.

6. Roll fondant to 1 PS thick. Cut three pieces to fit underside of brushes. Brush jam over cake and apply fondant. Cut three pieces to fit round sides of brushes. Brush thin film of jam over sponge and carefully apply fondant.

7. Make 1lb (450g) of fondant. Cover ½lb (220g) and color remainder brown. Roll to 2 PS thick. Cut to fit round cakes. Brush sponge with jam, then apply fondant, first the tops, then the bottoms, then sides.

8. Reserve 4oz (110g) white fondant and use remaining, plus trimmings, to make the tops of brushes, handles and lids for polish jars.

9. Roll to 1 PS thick, cut circles larger than tops of jars. Cut the first top white, then use combinations of color for remaining three. Secure with egg white. Score lids as shown with blunt edge of a knife.

10. Follow No. 9 for coloring. Cut brush tops (1 PS thick) larger than brushes. Secure with egg white. Roll fondant to 4 PS thick, cut handles ¾in. (20mm) wide and 4in. (100mm) long, with each end sloping. Bend around and secure with egg white. Leave all pieces overnight.

11. Make up the 8oz (220g) of royal icing. Using *No. 3 nozzle* pipe green lines around each side of cake. Pipe dots down each corner.

12. With *No. 2 nozzle* pipe a yellow line of dots and two lines inside green piping, then pipe dots along seams of green edging. Pipe **Shine your Shoes!** on the brush, as shown.

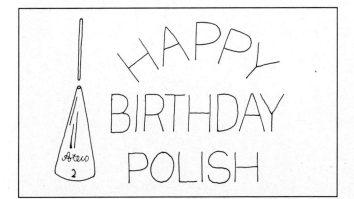

13. With *No. 1* carefully pipe brown bristles around brushes. Pipe green dots with *No. 2* around the tops of bristles. Using brown again and *No. 2* pipe **HAPPY BIRTHDAY** as shown, and **POLISH** on each jar. Pipe dots around the base of each jar. Pipe lines around handles of brushes.

14. Attach everything to main cake using dabs of icing to secure. Color the remaining 4oz (110g) of fondant with a little yellow and red. Roll to 1 PS thick and place loosely in center of cake, hanging over the edge, as shown.

Constant Telephone User

The rule in our house with regard to children using the telephone is: emergencies only; call at the "cheap rate" time; do not take longer than two minutes. The rule is constantly abused, so this cake was made with the children in mind.

The cake is simple to make and can be prepared in two days. The three circles of fondant which form the dial can be made by cutting around anything suitable —I used a baking pan for the largest, a beer glass for the next, and the base of an egg cup for the smallest.

Please read the General Notes on pages 6 to 9 before starting to decorate the cake. It is a good idea also to read through the step-by-step instructions and check the ingredients and equipment lists.

Ingredients for cake

12oz (340g) butter
9oz (250g) superfine sugar
15oz (420g) self-rising flour
9oz (250g) rice flour
9oz (250ml) milk beaten with 5 large eggs

flavoring (optional)
Make from this recipe: 1 × 7in. (180mm) square cake
1 × 1lb (450g) loaf cake—
approx. 7½in. (190mm) long

Ingredients for fondant and royal icing

1¾lb (780g) confectioner's sugar, plus 2oz (60g)
1¾ egg whites, plus ¼
almost 4 tblsp liquid glucose
flavoring (optional)
Also: warm sieved apricot jam; 50/50 mixture of cornstarch and confectioner's sugar in a dusting dredger; yellow, orange, and brown food coloring.

Equipment

Bowls for mixing icings; spoons; sifter; rolling pin; steel ruler; sharp-pointed knife; popsicle sticks (PS) as spacers; parchment paper for icing bags; pastry brush; Ateco (or equivalent) icing nozzles 2 and 3; 9in. (230mm) square silver board.

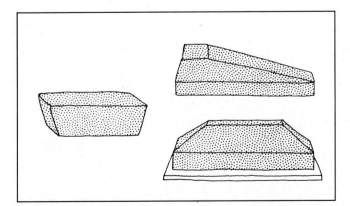

1. Having left the cakes overnight, slice the tops flat. Turn square cake upside down and cut sloping sides, as shown. Cut a slope at front, also as shown, leaving enough flat surface for loaf cake to sit on. Position cake in center of silver board.

2. Turn loaf cake upside down and round off all corners and edges. Cut piece out of base, as shown.

Make the 1¾lb (780g) of fondant and mix in yellow food coloring.

3. Brush base of loaf cake with warm jam. Roll a piece of fondant to 2 PS thick, cut to size, and carefully apply. Leave to dry.

4. Measure dimensions of large cake, then brush with jam. Roll fondant to 2 PS thick, cut to shape, then apply—first back, then sides, front and (in one piece) top and slope.

5. Keep a piece of yellow fondant, add orange to remainder. Dust a surface and place loaf cake fondant side down. Brush sponge with jam. Measure cake and roll fondant to 2 PS thick. Cut to shape and with help of rolling pin, apply fondant. Smooth over surface with hands. Leave to dry.

6. Take a piece of orange fondant and add brown. Roll to 4 PS thick and cut out two pieces ¾in. (20mm) wide to support receiver. Position on flat surface of large cake, securing with egg white.

7. Roll orange fondant to 2 PS thick, cut a circle 4½in. (110mm) in diameter. Leave to dry on a dusted surface. Add more yellow to yellow fondant, roll to 2 PS thick and cut a circle 3½in. (90mm) in diameter. Cut finger holes with small cutter—as many as number of letters in child's name, if possible.

8. Add more orange to small piece of orange fondant. Roll to 1 PS thick and cut circle to fit in center of dial. Leave all pieces to dry on a dusted surface for 2–3 hours.

9. When pieces are dry, brush center back of yellow dial with egg white and attach to large orange circle.
   Make up the 2oz (60g) of royal icing.

10. With *No. 3 nozzle* and orange icing, pipe lines of continuous dots on all seams of fondant on yellow cake and around base. Brush brown supports with egg white and attach receiver. Pipe continuous dots around bottom edge. Pipe age of child on smallest orange circle.

11. With *No. 2 nozzle* pipe **use this phone to call your friends** in bright orange, on top of receiver. (See notes on how to center lettering page 8.)

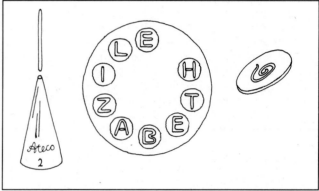

12. Using same nozzle and brown icing, pipe name of child, or something else appropriate, in finger holes. Stick small orange circle onto center of dial with a swirl of piped icing. Stick completed dial onto telephone, again with piped icing, pressing gently to secure.

13. Using same nozzle and icing, pipe a second line of continuous dots around base of telephone.
   Roll fondant trimmings into a ball and add brown.

14. Make a sausage long enough to go from the side of the receiver to back of telephone. Flatten each end a little, then attach with egg white—hold until secure. Pipe three lines of continuous dots, using *nozzle No. 3*, around both joints.

Vehicles

London Bus

Apart from the piping (straight lines!) this is one of the simplest cakes to make. It can be completed in a day and a half, although windows, etc., are easier to apply if the red fondant has been left overnight to dry.

Piping lines is easy to do once you get used to holding the bag and controlling the flow of icing. Practice on your kitchen table if this cake is your first attempt. The introductory notes for the Shoe Polishing cake may help with the piping of letters and numbers.

Please read the General Notes on pages 6 to 9 before starting to decorate the cake. Also read through the step-by-step instructions and check the ingredients and equipment lists.

Ingredients for cake

8oz (220g) butter
6oz (170g) superfine sugar
10oz (280g) self-rising flour
6oz (170g) rice flour
5oz (140ml) milk beaten with 3 large eggs
filling

Make from this recipe:
1 × 1lb (450g) loaf cake
1 × 2lb (900g) loaf cake

Ingredients for fondant and royal icing

1lb (450g) confectioner's sugar, plus 4oz (110g)
1 egg white, plus ½
2 tblsp liquid glucose
flavoring (optional)
Also: warm sieved apricot jam; 50/50 mixture of corn-starch and confectioner's sugar in a dusting dredger; bright red, yellow and black food coloring.

Equipment

Bowls for mixing icings; sifter; spoons; rolling pin; steel ruler; sharp-pointed knife; popsicle sticks (PS) as spacers; pastry brush; parchment paper for icing bags; Ateco (or equivalent) icing nozzles 1, 2 and 3; 9in. (230mm) square silver board.

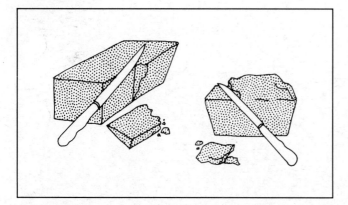

1. Having left the cakes overnight, slice the top and sloping sides of the 2lb (900g) cake so that it becomes a square-sided oblong. Slice the top from the 1lb (450g) cake and neaten the sloping sides.

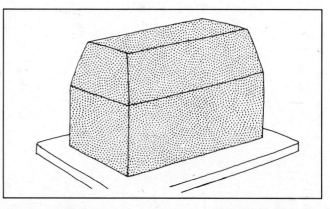

2. Turn smaller cake upside down. Sandwich the two cakes together with buttercream and/or jam. Position in center of silver board.

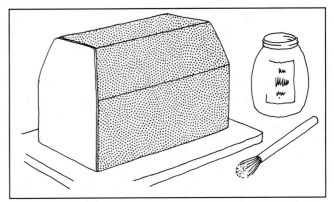

3. Make 1lb (450g) fondant. Put 3oz (80g) on one side (covered) and color remaining fondant bright red. Measure dimensions of cake, then roll fondant to 2 PS thick.

4. Cut front and back pieces first. Brush cake with jam, then carefully apply fondant. Cut side pieces, brush cake with jam, apply fondant. Cut top and repeat the above. Trim edges if necessary.

5. Take a little red fondant. Roll to 1 PS thick and cut four circles ⅝ in. (15mm) in diameter. These go in center of wheels.

6. Add drops of black coloring to some of red fondant. Roll to 4 PS thick and cut four circles 1¼ in. (30mm) in diameter. Mark a tread around the edges with blunt side of a knife.
   If possible, leave everything to dry overnight.

7. Take 2oz (60g) of remaining white fondant, add a little black coloring. Roll to 1 PS thick and cut strips ¾ in. (20mm) wide. Cut windows and doors as shown.

8. The two front windows are slightly larger than the others. Round off corners of windows where indicated. Carefully brush backs with egg white and apply to bus. Position wheels using egg white, then apply red circles in centers.

9. Roll white fondant to 1 PS thick and cut two headlights ¼ in. (6mm) diameter. Brush backs with egg white and position under large front windows. Cut a ½ in. (12mm) square, cut off corners and position above front window.

10. Use remaining fondant, adding yellow coloring to some, to make bus signs. Roll the fondant to 1 PS thick. The signs can be applied before or after the lettering has been piped.

11. Make up the 4oz (110g) of royal icing, add enough black coloring to make medium gray. With *No. 2 nozzle* pipe around the edges of windows and door, as shown.

12. Mix some black into the icing to make darker gray. Still using *No. 2* pipe dark gray dots along seams of red fondant—around top edge and down front. Pipe other markings on bus as shown, then pipe number of bus—child's age.

13. With dark gray and *No. 1 nozzle* pipe details on windows, windshield wipers, circles on headlights and details on signs.

14. On front sign pipe **London**; on back sign **LONDON**; on one side **HAPPY BIRTHDAY**; on the other **LONDON SIGHTSEEING TOUR**. Finally, with a *No. 3 nozzle* pipe a line (avoiding wheels) around base of bus. The words above can be used to trace from—see page 8 for instructions on how to center.

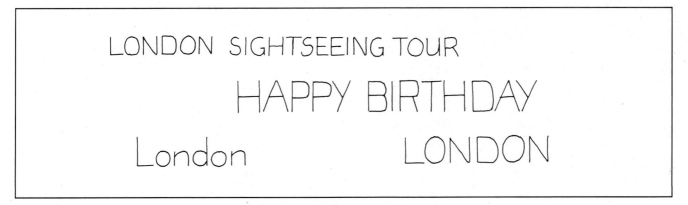

The sample words above can be used to trace from – see
the introductory notes on page 9, on how to centre.

Race Track

When this cake was made I was unable to obtain the correct size silver board: I taped four 8in. (200mm) boards together with cellophane tape and the fondant roads were layed to cover up the joints (but they do give the cake a little more interest).

The cars on the track are based on "Formula Fords," the lowest of the Formula cars in which most racers begin their careers (they are also the easiest to model).

The cake can be prepared in three days. Please read the General Notes on pages 6 to 9 before starting. It is also a good idea to read through the step-by-step instructions and check the ingredients and equipment lists.

Ingredients for cake

12oz (340g) butter
9oz (250g) superfine sugar
15oz (420g) self-rising flour
9oz (250g) rice flour
9oz (250ml) milk beaten with 5 large eggs
buttercream for filling

Make from this recipe: 1 × 7in. (180mm) round cake
 1 × 2lb (900g) loaf cake

Ingredients for fondant and royal icing

2½lb (1.120kg) confectioner's sugar, plus 6oz (170g)
2½ egg whites, plus ¾
5 tblsp liquid glucose
flavoring (optional)
Also: warm sieved apricot jam; 50/50 mixture of cornstarch and confectioner's sugar in a dusting dredger; green, black, silver, yellow, red and blue food coloring.

Equipment

Bowls for mixing icings; spoons; rolling pin; steel ruler; sharp-pointed knife; popsicle sticks (PS) as spacers; pastry brush; paintbrush; parchment paper for icing bags; 2¼in. (55mm) round cutter; ⁵⁄₈in. (15mm) round cutter; Ateco (or equivalent) icing nozzles 1, 3 and 9; 16in. (400mm) square silver board.

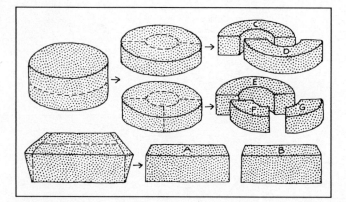

1. Having left the cakes overnight, slice the tops flat. Slice the round cake in half. Cut away sloping sides from loaf cake, then cut in half lengthways. Press large cutter in center of both round cakes, then cut each cake in half, and one half in half again, as shown.

2. Position pieces on board, as shown. Cut remaining half of loaf cake to fit spaces, then cut a sloping piece to go inside track. Go round track with knife, leveling surfaces and neatening joints. Stick all pieces together with buttercream. Make the 2½lb (1.120kg) of fondant. Color 2¼lb (1kg) green.

3. Brush inside walls of track with warm jam. Measure height of wall and then roll fondant to 2 PS thick. Cut into manageable pieces and apply. Repeat with outside walls. Cut roads to fit where indicated, 2 PS thick and 1in. (25mm) wide. Attach to board with egg white.

4. Add black to green trimmings to make gray. Brush top of track with jam. Apply as before, cutting fondant roughly to shape, then trimming after application. Add more black to some of trimmings for tunnels. Roll to 1 PS thick and cut three circles with large cutter. Cut in half and apply where indicated.

5. Make the 6oz (170g) of royal icing. With *No. 3 nozzle* and green icing, pipe continuous dots along track edges, then around base and tunnels. Pipe black continuous dots along edges of roads on board. With *No. 1* and white icing, pipe markings on track, as shown (pipe a line across fondant joints).

6. Add blue to some gray trimmings and model two cars as shown, 5 PS thick and about 2in. (50mm) long, ½in. (12mm) wide. Add black to remaining trimmings. Roll to 3 PS thick and cut thirty-two wheels with small cutter. Make indent in each center with *No. 9 nozzle*, then paint silver. Leave on dusted surface.

7. Using remaining white fondant, model six more cars in different colors (break a little piece from each color and make six helmets, as shown). Leave to dry for an hour.

8. Attach wheels and helmets to cars, using egg white. With *No. 1 nozzle* and white icing, pipe goggles on helmets. Using different colored icing, pipe lines on helmets, then numbers and lines on cars. Leave for 30 minutes, then attach to track with egg white.

Train

I thought a boxcar or truck full of jolly pink pigs would be a change from the usual sweets or chocolates. It would be fun to have the pigs in different flavors, say strawberry, banana, lemon and orange—the flavoring should not make any difference to the color.

As it is impossible to buy a cake board to fit the train, I had to join two 8in. (200mm) boards. Tape the boards on top and underneath, using a clear cellophane tape.

The cake can be prepared in two days, but three days would be better. Please read the General Notes on pages 6 to 9 before you start. Also read through the step-by-step instructions and check the ingredients and equipment lists.

Ingredients for cake

10oz (280g) butter
8oz (220g) superfine sugar
13oz (360g) self-rising flour
7oz (200g) rice flour
8oz (220ml) milk beaten with 4 large eggs

Make from this recipe: 1 × 8in. (200mm) square cake
2 × 5oz (140g) food-can cakes

Ingredients for fondant and royal icing

3lb (1.340kg) confectioner's sugar, plus 4oz (110g)
3 egg whites, plus ½
6 tblsp liquid glucose
flavoring (optional)
Also: warm sieved apricot jam; 50/50 mixture of cornstarch and confectioner's sugar in a dusting dredger; yellow, blue and red food coloring; edible silver balls.

Equipment

Bowls for mixing icings; sifter; spoons; rolling pin; steel ruler; sharp-pointed knife; popsicle sticks (PS) as spacers; pastry brush; paintbrush; parchment paper for icing bags; Ateco (or equivalent) icing nozzle 2; 2¼in. (60mm) round cutter; 2 × 8in. (200mm) square silver cake boards; clear cellophane tape.

1. Having left the cakes overnight, slice the tops flat. Cut square cake in half. Cut a 2½in. (60mm) piece from one half, rounding off one of top edges, as shown. Cut one of little cakes to 2in. (50mm) high, and round off top. Attach cabin to engine with jam and/or buttercream.

2. Make the 3lb (1.340kg) of fondant (in two batches for ease). Position engine at slight angle on board. Color 1¼lb (560g) of fondant pale yellow. Measure dimensions, then brush with jam. Roll fondant to 2 PS thick, cut each piece to size and apply: sides, front, top of body and front of cabin.

3. Cut top of cabin and back in one piece. Make a hook, as shown, and attach to back with egg white. Roll trimmings to 2 PS thick and cut four circles with cutter. Leave on a dusted surface. Color 1lb (450g) of fondant pale blue. Position boxcar on board. Cover as before: back, front, sides, then top.

4. Roll fondant to 2 PS thick and cut five more wheels. Roll a small piece, place around hook and attach to front of boxcar with egg white. Measure circumference of chimney, then brush with jam. Cut fondant (2 PS thick) and apply. Position on engine, using jam to secure.

5. Brush top of chimney with jam and apply one of blue wheels. Brush top and sides of dome. Cover top, with newly cut yellow wheel, and sides as for chimney.

6. Add blue trimmings to about 3oz (80g) of white. Roll to 4 PS thick and cut strips ³/₈ in. (10mm) wide to go around top of carriage. Attach with egg white. Add a little red to remaining white fondant. Model pigs' heads, as shown. Attach ears and noses with egg white. Mark smile with blunt edge of knife.

7. Position each head in carriage while still soft. Attach silver balls with dabs of egg white. Put a little fondant underneath two heads at front to give impression of bodies. Slice back of seventh head and attach to window.

8. Make the 4oz (110g) of royal icing. Color half blue, half yellow. Pipe continuous dots along all fondant seams and around base of cakes. Pipe lines on cabin top and on wheels, as shown. After 30 minutes, attach wheels to engine and carriage, using egg white to secure.

Seasonal

Halloween

Halloween (All Hallow Eve) was a feast originally celebrated by the Celts as the eve of their new year. Fires were lit to ensure new life after the winter. In later times, ghosts and witches were thought to roam the earth and the fires were built to keep them away. Burning candles in pumpkins is said to come from an Irish legend: A man called Jack was barred from heaven because of his meanness. As he had nowhere to go, he walked the earth (along with the ghosts and goblins) carrying a lantern. "Trick or Treat" is a fairly recent innovation. Children go from house to house, in costume, asking for a treat—fruit, money or candy. If the treat is forthcoming, they promise not to play a trick.

When all the cake ingredients have been blended, divide the mixture between the two pans, putting quite a bit more in one than the other. The cake can be prepared in two to three days. Please read the General Notes on pages 6 to 9 before starting. Also read through the step-by-step instructions and check the ingredients and equipment lists.

Ingredients for cake

12oz (340g) butter

9oz (250g) superfine sugar
15oz (420g) self-rising flour
9oz (250g) rice flour
9oz (250ml) milk beaten with 5 large eggs
Make from this recipe: 2 × 7in. (180mm) round cakes

Ingredients for fondant and royal icing

1½lb (670g) confectioner's sugar, plus 4oz (110g)
1½ egg whites, plus ½
3 tblsp liquid glucose
flavoring (optional)
Also: warm sieved apricot jam; 50/50 mixture of cornstarch and confectioner's sugar in a dusting dredger; blue, black, flesh, silver and yellow coloring.

Equipment

Bowls for mixing icings; sifter; spoons; rolling pin; sharp-pointed knife; popsicle sticks (PS) as spacers; pastry brush; parchment paper for icing bags; Ateco (or equivalent) icing nozzles 1, 2, 3, 7 and 15; small star cutter; 2¼in. (55mm) round cutter; 10in. (250mm) round silver cake board.

1. Having left the cakes overnight, slice the tops flat. Cut a 1in. (25mm) piece from the thinner cake and ³⁄₈in. (15mm) from the other, as shown. Make the 1½lb (670g) of fondant. Brush thicker cake with jam and position toward front of silver board. Take 12oz (340g) of fondant and roll to 2 PS thick.

2. With help of a rolling pin, cover thicker cake (apart from cut piece at back). Add 8oz (220g) of fondant to trimmings and color darkish blue. Apply to thinner cake (apart from cut piece) as before. Leave on dusted surface. Break off two-thirds of trimmings, add black, then put aside.

3. Make the 4oz (110g) of royal icing. Color some brown. With *No. 7 nozzle* pipe a line across blue cake, as shown. With *No. 2* pipe broom head, as shown.

Roll some white fondant trimmings to 1 PS thick, cut four stars and a half moon. Leave on dusted surface.

4. Take 4oz (110g) of fondant and color yellow. Shape into three balls. Make a hole in each center, then mark grooves with blunt edge of knife. Stick in white candles. Leave on dusted surface.

Take a little fondant and add flesh. Model face and hands of witch (face flat on one side).

5. Add warts to nose and chin (poor lady!). Attach head to cake and hands to broomstick, using egg white. Mark fingers with knife. With black fondant, model witch pieces, as shown. Attach short arm to cake first, then body, then top arm. Model the hat and brim. Stick together, leave on dusted surface.

6. With *No. 1 nozzle* and dark gray icing, pipe eye, brow and curly hair. Position leg and shoe. Roll black fondant to 1 PS. Cut skirt, as shown, and attach.

Make three large and three smaller balls (for cats). Cut in half and stick to sides of white cake with egg white.

7. Stand blue cake upright and brush back with jam. Roll fondant trimmings to 1 PS thick. Lay cake on fondant. Carefully lift and position, with jam, at back of white cake. Attach pumpkins to cake with egg white.

8. With blue icing and *No. 15 nozzle*, pipe stars around base and part of top edge of white cake. Paint stars and moon silver and attach with egg white. With *No. 1* and dark gray icing, pipe eyes, whiskers and ears on cats. Use *No. 3* to pipe tails.

Christmas Eve

This is one of my favorite cakes. Having manoeuvered his way down the chimney and safely delivered the seasonal gifts, Santa Claus now finds himself stuck—the mince pies and sherry must have added a few inches to his waistline.

The cake can be decorated in two days. Please read General Notes on pages 6 to 9 before starting. Also read through the step-by-step instructions and check the ingredients and equipment lists.

Ingredients for cake

16oz (450g) butter
12oz (340g) superfine sugar
20oz (560g) self-rising flour
12oz (340g) rice flour
10oz (280ml) milk beaten with 6 large eggs
buttercream for filling
Make from this recipe: 2 × 7in. (180mm) square cakes

Ingredients for fondant and royal icing

3lb (1.340kg) confectioner's sugar, plus 1oz (30g)
3 egg whites, plus $1/8$
6 tblsp liquid glucose
flavoring (optional)
Also: warm sieved apricot jam; 50/50 mixture of cornstarch and confectioner's sugar in a dusting dredger; black, red, brown, green, yellow and blue food coloring.

Equipment

Bowls for mixing icings; sifter; spoons; rolling pin; steel ruler; sharp-pointed knife; popsicle sticks (PS) as spacers; pastry brush; $5/8$ in. (15mm) round cutter; parchment paper for icing bags; Ateco (or equivalent) icing nozzle 1; small paintbrush; 10in. (250mm) square silver board.

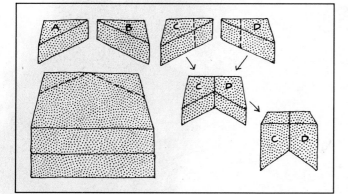

1. Having left the cakes overnight, slice the tops flat. Put one cake on top of other, measure 3½in. (90mm) up each side and cut to top middle point, as shown. Take two of remaining pieces and cut off 1½in. (40mm), as shown (the larger pieces join to make the chimney).

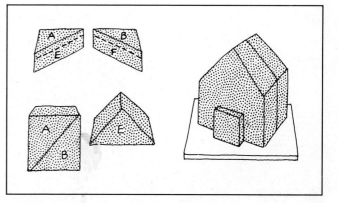

2. Slice a third from the two remaining pieces. The two thin pieces will join to make porch (trim to make a 3in. [75mm] square). One of the deep pieces will be the porch roof. Sandwich main house and porch together with buttercream. Position, at an angle, on silver cake board.

3. Make 2lb (900g) of fondant and color gray. Measure house back then brush with jam. Roll fondant to 2 PS thick, cut to size and carefully apply. Mark stones with blunt edge of knife. Repeat process of covering for both sides of porch, porch (in one piece) and gable end, marking stones after each application.

4. Cover base of porch roof with fondant 1 PS thick. Brush back and base with jam and position on top of porch. Roll fondant to 2 PS thick, cut to fit front porch roof, apply and mark stones.

5. Measure dimensions of roofs then brush with jam. Roll fondant to 1 PS thick, cut to size, then carefully apply, Join chimney pieces together with jam and a layer of fondant. Leave to dry (overnight if possible).

6. Make the 1oz (30g) of royal icing. Measure sides of chimney, then brush with jam. Roll fondant to 2 PS thick, cut to fit, then apply. Stand chimney upside down and mark stones. Brush inside sponge with jam, then dab icing along inside joint. Carefully position on roof.

7. Make 1lb (450g) of fondant. Brush top of chimney with jam. Take 4oz (110g) of fondant, flatten with hands and apply to chimney, pushing it gently down sides. Color some fondant pale yellow, roll to 1 PS thick and cut three oblong windows roughly 1¾ in. (45mm) long and 1¼ in.(30mm) wide; and two round windows.

8. Paint brown leading on windows. Brush backs with egg white, attach round windows to each side of porch, others to each wall of house. Roll some green fondant to 1 PS thick, cut a door and shutters for oblong windows, mark grooves while still soft. Brush backs with egg white, then apply.

9. Make brown fondant, roll to 2 PS thick, cut sills for windows (half-circles for round ones) and frame for door. Brush with egg white and apply. Take white fondant, brush tops of windows with egg white and attach snow.

10. Take gray trimmings. Cut in two, add green to half and blue with a little yellow to other half. Roll to 1 PS thick and cut tiles about $^5/_8$ in. (15mm) in diameter. Starting at bottom edge, apply with egg white to both roofs, stopping $^3/_4$ in. (20mm) from top ridge.

11. Using soft white fondant cover roof ridges and around base of house, as shown. Color about 6oz (170g) of fondant red and some flesh, for hands and head. Model hands and head, as shown. Stick hands to chimney and mark fingers with blunt edge of knife.

12. Model body and arms, as shown. Position, with head, securing with dabs of egg white. Model a hood—a flat triange—and attach to head. Roll some white fondant and attach around hood and sleeve edges.

13. Make a little pink nose and attach to face. Press two small white balls flat and attach to face, for eyes. Repeat with red fondant for mouth. Paint eyes with blue coloring, as shown.

14. With *No. 1 nozzle* and white icing, pipe beard and eyebrows. Pipe icicles hanging from some roof tiles—press nozzle gently into tile, let some icing come, then pull sharply. With brown icing pipe handles on door, windows and shutters, then hinges on shutters.